On Schillhammer Road

the life of a botanist

Hubert W. Vogelmann

Foreword by
Charles W. Johnson

The Tamarac Press • Warren, Vermont
August 2011

"On Ice" was originally published in *Vermont Life*, 1995; "Splitting Wood" was orginally published in *Northern Woodlands,* 2004; "Spring Begins in January" was orginally published as "Spring Begins the Third Week in January" in *Northern Woodlands,* 2006. "Catastrophe on Camels Hump" is reprinted from *Natural History Magazine,* 1982.

Photographs are from the Hubert W. Vogelmann collection at the Bailey/Howe Library, University of Vermont, or provided by the Vogelmann family.

Line drawings by Hub Vogelmann.

Cover design by Jonathan Draudt Design/Tamarac Arts, Warren, VT. Cover photograph by Jonathan Draudt: Sparganium eurycarpum

ISBN: 978-0-9706620-3-3

Published in Warren, Vermont, by The Tamarac Press.
www.thetamaracpress.com

In loving memory of my wife, Marie,
who shared her life with a botanist

Contents

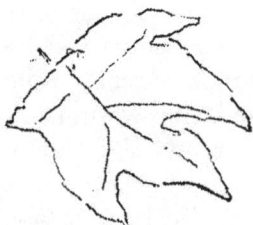

Foreword

Charles W. Johnson, BA, MS, PhD
Vermont State Naturalist, 1978 – 2000

Even before I met him almost forty years ago, Hub Vogelmann's reputation preceded him. He was known widely in Vermont and beyond as a respected field botanist and cornerstone at the University of Vermont, a selfless teacher, a passionate conservationist, and a man of unusual modesty who willingly shares his knowledge of—and delight in—the natural world. I even heard someone describe him as "a rarity—a botanist with charisma."

When I did get to know him, as his graduate student and colleague, I experienced all these qualities first-hand. But even more, I found Hub to be a gentleman who treated everyone with respect, kindness, and patience—attributes that served him well over so many years in multiple roles as teacher, advisor, administrator, and even the reluctant celebrity he became through his research.

Now, years after his formal "retirement" from the University of Vermont (yet hardly from his many interests and activities), we all, even those who never met him, are given the opportunity to know him through his own written words. The title of his book, On Schillhammer Road: the life of a botanist, captures perfectly what I believe Hub intended with this work: a personal rendering of a life lived close to home and close to nature, each reinforcing the other, bringing real meaning and satisfaction. As a work of non-fiction, it is hard to classify or pigeon-hole, for it is part memoir, part observations of the goings-on outside, part reflections on the human condition (plus and minus), and part overview of the ecological research that drew sometimes-unwelcome renown.

Since it is all of that in just over two hundred pages, each part must necessarily be brief and somewhat circumscribed, yet taken together they give us the essence of what motivates him, what he sees and feels and thinks, what he values. All of that is worth knowing and leaves us wanting to know more about him and about the world he entices us to experience—especially so when we realize we are in the company of a man whose research on Camel's Hump catapulted the concept of acid precipitation and its environmental effects into the public consciousness, where it remains today as one of the planet's huge environmental issues.

On Schillhammer Road takes us on many field trips with Hub as personal guide and interpreter. Some trips are far away treks (Europe, Colombia, the Arctic), where he went in search of adventure, education, or research. But most are not so far at all—just down the road from his house or in his back pastures, where we stroll in his easy company as he points to everyday observations of things or events that bring him pleasure and solidify his connection to the place he calls home.

I especially love his descriptions of little discoveries he makes in these daily sojourns, ordinary things and events we often overlook but which to him are exciting glimpses into the marvels of nature. A few neat examples: Colorado potato beetles seem to prefer red varieties of potatoes over white; a chipmunk can stuff as many as 105 sunflower seeds in its cheek pouches; wild leeks have contractile roots that pull the bulbs deeper into the ground; his indicator for the "crossover" of spring to summer is when dandelions stop blooming and buttercups begin.

This is a most accessible book. It is not intellectually lofty or overstuffed with details. It is not wrought with thinly-disguised self-promotion. Rather, in its unadorned, direct way, it imparts selected but important bits of information while conveying Hub's awe of and reverence for the natural world, the wellspring for his life and work. It speaks with love, unabashed but never sentimental, for his family, who, in various ways, are now carrying on his legacy. With a freshness and charming innocence, he writes of boyhood experiences in nature that set the stage for the life he was to lead, things we all can relate to. With a guileless kind of humor, he relates brief stories about friends, neighbors, and associates who have shared moments or decades with him along the way.

He expends little, if any, ink on his own accomplishments, such as having been head of the UVM Botany Department, curator of the Pringle Herbarium, author of two booklets that prompted protection of important natural areas in Vermont, founder of the state's chapter of The Nature Conservancy, a key figure in the passage of Vermont's landmark environmental law Act 250, stimulus behind thousands of acres of Camels Hump State Park being designated a Research Natural Area and National Natural Landmark, creator of UVM's nationally recognized graduate Field Naturalist Program, and many others. Even when discussing the research at Camels Hump that brought him into the national and international spotlight, he downplays his own role and importance. Of course, this is Hub's way. He does not make noise or draw attention to himself.

No, in this book, as in his life, he is not a big boulder dropped into a lake, making a loud splash and sending waves careening out. He is more the gentle rain upon the water, the drops touching softly before blending in, their ripples expanding until they eventually cover the entire surface.

Preface

THE LIFE OF A BOTANIST

After thirty-six years teaching botany at the University of Vermont, I retired in 1991. At this turning point in my life, I began to explore writing, finding a variety of subjects that interested me, especially things I noticed going on in the natural world. When the opportunity arose, I went to a writing workshop conducted by the University of Vermont's Writing Across the Curriculum Program, which further sparked my interest. My colleague, Gale Lawrence, who also attended the workshop, encouraged me to do more.

I enjoy thinking about what I see in the natural world and I like writing about what I think. The thoughts may be about plants, animals, the weather—whatever catches my attention at the time—and it seems fitting to set those observations down.

Gale's curiosity about why and how I became a botanist motivated me to write a series of autobiographical snapshots to tell as much of my life story as was needed to explain the decision to come to UVM and settle in Vermont. I then turned to the subjects that interest me most—facts and observations about plants and animals, especially those I observe where I live on Schillhammer Road in Jericho, Vermont. At times, I reflect on how I came to be where I am, given where I started out.

For as far back as I can remember, I have especially enjoyed discoveries about the little things in nature, like how many sunflower seeds a chipmunk can hold in its cheeks (105) and how fast a woolly bear caterpillar crawls (two feet a minute). While these are not earth shaking discoveries, they help us to understand more about life in the natural world.

Sometimes little observations grow into important discoveries. Hiking in the mountains of Vermont in the 1960's, I observed that when a cloud moved into the forest, tiny water droplets were combed from the fog and collected onto the needles of spruces and firs, and the droplets fell to the ground like rainfall. Wondering how significant this was, I set about capturing fog with window screens and found that an amazing amount of water settled out. This simple observation demonstrated the role of fog in replenishing ground water and feeding mountain streams. Over the course of time, other experiments revealed how fog's elevated acid level contributed to heightened tree mortality at higher elevations, where fog is a common phenomenon. Essays on Camel's Hump and Acid Rain provide a window onto the bitter political controversy that took hold around this fact of science.

But, first, my little discovery led me to Mexico, where my experiments on fog capture showed that fog in the mountains of eastern Mexico was the most important source of water during the dry season of the year. As a result of these pioneering studies, I was given a Certificate of Appreciation from an international body of scientists who held a fog moisture conference, the First International Conference on Fog and Fog Collection, in Vancouver, Canada, in 1998. Little observations can lead to big discoveries.

Looking back over thirty-six years of teaching and research at UVM, I think of those parts of my career that caused it to be, for better or worse, what it came to be. Perhaps the most important influence in shaping my teaching and research life has been my students. Both singly and collectively, they have made all the difference, coming to me with unfettered minds and innovative suggestions that shaped my research. Without their input and labors, I could not have begun to accomplish what I did. Indeed, the most important discoveries in my own research came from the ideas of my students, both graduate and undergraduate, and especially Thomas Siccama, whose long-term research on the forests of Camel's Hump propelled our work into the national and international spotlight on issues surrounding acid rain.

Over the years, I've been involved more than once in what seemed like local activities that turned out to have a reach far beyond my own community of scientists and students. Acid rain, The Nature

Conservancy, the Field Naturalist Program at the University of Vermont, all have their own impact on the world, some greater than I could have predicted at their outset. Here again, I'm fascinated with how the small act of an organism—me—interacts with the world it's a part of, while remaining just a man living on Schillhammer Road who likes to observe the natural world.

Even now, long after my so-called retirement, I see something new every day, whether it is a flower I had not seen before, or a chipmunk hiding in his burrow, or a woodpecker hammering away at a tree branch. Perhaps it is an obsession, but the how and why of these things have always been part of my everyday life.

There was no grand plan for my writings, and the thought of writing a book was far from my mind at the outset. However, after I had written a substantial collection of essays, Gale suggested I might have enough material for a book. I also participate in a monthly writing group, and they too encouraged me to think about publishing. And so the hard work of crafting this book began.

I begin with a chapter on my early years in Buffalo, New York. Following chapters trace my education, professional life, and life on Schillhammer Road in Jericho, Vermont, where I raised vegetables and Black Angus. Throughout, I have always sought the adventure of exploration and discovery. These explorations are included here, also, along with some observations about Vermont's changing seasons.

And the final section deals with the research on Camel's Hump mountain, investigating the effect of acid rain on the forest, which received international attention.

Hub Vogelmann
December 2010

On
Schillhammer Road

I.
Beginnings

Born in Buffalo

Once in a while I get a flashback to my early years in Buffalo. In my earliest recollection I was perhaps two or three years old. My father was a United Church of Christ minister, and our family was often involved in church suppers and other affairs that kept us out late into the evening. We lived on Chamberlain Drive in South Buffalo about three miles from the church. I recall my father driving home late at night with me half asleep in the back seat of our Studebaker. When we turned off the main road onto Chamberlain Drive, there was a loose manhole cover that clanged as the wheels rode over it, giving me a warm feeling as I realized I would soon be home in my comfortable bed.

When I was five years old, we moved from Chamberlain Drive to Byer Place about a mile away. Here two trees stood in the yard and a golf course was across the road. I can't remember much about our home on Byer Place except that we had a cat named Bingo who was black with a white spot on her throat. But I do remember Sunday afternoons.

On Sunday afternoons my father would often take my brother and me to the Buffalo Museum of Science. The museum offered beautifully presented programs on nature that filled my childhood world with dreams. I vividly recall a documentary film on life in a marsh where red-winged blackbirds clung to cattail stalks and made their raspy calls. It was an emotional experience for me, and even today I feel the tug of that film when I see a redwing. I feel it again when I see a V of geese flying south in autumn.

I can also remember the first time my father took me fishing. I couldn't have been more than five years old when he drove me to the

Niagara River near Buffalo, handed me a baited rod, and sat with me on the river bank. I don't remember if I caught anything, but I recall the anxious look on his face as he sat there, hoping I would. When my father was not preaching or tending to his flock, he was fishing. It could be in the Niagara River or on Lake Erie or on a quiet lake in the Adirondacks or Canada. We never took a vacation where my father couldn't fish. As busy as he was, he often fished at night on Lake Erie, using a lantern to light the way for his boat. At home we ate fish, fish, and more fish. My mother learned to cook whatever he caught many different ways—fried, boiled, baked, souped, chowdered, pickled, and more.

Recognizing my father's passion for fishing, his congregation gave him a plaque inscribed with the angler's prayer. It read, "Lord give me grace to catch a fish so big that even I, when telling of it afterwards, would never need to lie." That plaque hung in our entryway as long as I can remember. My father's best fishing friend was the local undertaker, Mr. Geistorfer. Like my father, he could tell fishing stories endlessly. One night at the dinner table, my father told about a large funeral he and Mr. Geistorfer conducted that day. My father rode in the hearse with Mr. Geistorfer, leading a long column of cars accompanied by police on motorcycles to the cemetery. They were so engrossed in their fishing stories that they drove the hearse right past the cemetery entrance with all the cars and motorcycles following close behind. When they realized what they had done they stopped, but the entire procession had to back up to clear the entrance and let the hearse through. How embarrassing.

Every summer our family rented a cottage on Halls Lake, a Canadian trout-fishing spot about fifty miles north of Toronto. My uncle rented a cottage nearby and each morning and night he and my father fished for trout. They were so dedicated they would fish in rainstorms and in winds so strong they had to take extra care that their boat didn't tip over. I would meet the boat when they came ashore and offer to clean the fish. It was slimy, smelly work, but I sort of enjoyed the mindless task that freed my thoughts for other things. And my father and uncle gave me encouraging praise because they didn't want to do it themselves.

One day they came ashore with six beautiful lake trout. My young cousin saw the fish hanging from the stringer and thought they looked dry. He asked for permission to row the boat into deeper water so he could dip the fish and wet them. That he did, but the stringer slipped from his hand and down it went to the bottom of Halls Lake. After that he wasn't the popular kid anymore, but I didn't have to clean that particular catch.

Finally my parents bought a house, their first, on Tuscarora Road. Living on a minister's meager salary, they were happy to have accumulated enough wealth to buy their own home. Although our address was on Tuscarora Road, our lot ended at a slanting intersection with Shenandoah Road, which meant our yard was pie-shaped. It narrowed in the back yard, where it ended between our garage and that of our neighbor.

The space between these structures was no more than fifteen feet but this "wasted" space became important to me, for it was here my life as a naturalist began.

As a boy of ten, I felt compelled to collect anything that was alive. For some reason I was drawn to pigeons. I thought they were beautiful and yearned to raise them. We had been in our new home about a year when I built a pigeon coop in the space between the garages. There was no money for lumber, but nearby mills let me have the old packing crates that machinery had arrived in. My father hauled the wood in his Studebaker to our Tuscarora home. Pulling nails and sorting through the broken boards, I managed to salvage enough to build a small coop.

The coop was about five feet by five feet but had enough head room for me to stand up inside. I built four nesting boxes along one wall about a foot from the ceiling and left an entrance in the front wall where the pigeons could enter and leave. Since pigeons have homing instincts, I had to keep my first pairs inside the coop until they laid eggs and hatched their young, establishing this as their new home base. I would sit on a stool near the nests and watch their every move. My greatest enjoyment came when the first broods were able to fly—now I could let them leave the coop to fly free and return. It was even more fun to put my pigeons in a cage, get my father to drive to the country twenty-five miles from the city, release them and see whether they or I could get back to the coop first. They always won and I marveled then, as I do today, at how they could find their way.

After my early years with pigeons, I decided to raise rabbits, so I converted the pigeon coop into a rabbit hutch, dividing it into several compartments. With the new design I could no longer sit inside to watch, but I still enjoyed observing my rabbits, and they sure knew how to reproduce! Disposing of the growing rabbit population was a constant problem, and I eventually gave all of them away.

Honeybees came shortly after I got rid of the rabbits. My father bought the necessary parts for a hive and purchased a package of bees from one of his parishioners. I assembled the hive and we set it behind our house, placing it halfway between our neighbors' houses to give as much clearance from flying bees as possible. Although my father loved the idea of getting honey from the bees, he was afraid to work with them and they became my responsibility. But I loved it all. I would sit near the hive entrance and watch the bees come and go. They carried pollen of many different colors on their legs, and I wondered where in this city they could possibly find enough flowers to gather all the pollen and nectar they needed.

Problems with our neighbors arose during the first year. It started in early spring when the bees that had overwintered in the hive made their first flight, called a cleansing flight. During this particular event, the bees excrete brown poop that falls on everything within flying range. When our neighbors hung white sheets on the line on warm sunny days, which were also perfect days for cleansing flights, the recently washed sheets suddenly looked as if they had the measles. The remedy was moving our bee colony onto the porch roof in front of our house so the cleansing flights didn't include flying over the neighbors' clotheslines.

The only way I could get out to the porch roof was to squeeze through a window in my parents' bedroom. One corner of the room served as my father's study, where a small desk with an ancient Underwood typewriter stood in front of the window. My father would sit and peck out his sermons on that typewriter for delivery, word for word, to his polite congregation on Sunday mornings. When I came to visit the bees—about twice a week—he had to slide his desk and typewriter out of the way so I could climb out the window. But he never complained. He was delighted that I was taking such good care of his bees. Keeping our bees on the roof helped relations with our neighbors, but there were still scattered episodes of dirty sheets every spring.

My father shared some of my naturalist interests and often talked about his dream of raising things and living off the land. He fell in love with a book called *Five Acres and Independence: A Handbook for Small Farm Management*, by M. G. Kains. Each night at supper, my father would talk about what he had just read—how many berries, apples, tomatoes, or whatever you could grow on just a few acres.

During the World War II years when I was a teenager, patriotic citizens were asked to raise their own vegetables in Victory Gardens. What a wonderful excuse to get rid of that miserable, weedy lawn in our back yard. It never grew good grass anyway. So we turned the turf over and exposed a sandy soil that looked as if it might once have been a beach during an ancient Lake Erie or glacial episode. We went ahead and planted two dwarf cherries along one property line and set a plum in front of my old pigeon coop/rabbit hutch. The rest of the yard went to vegetables. In spite of the poor acidic soil, we grew wonderful strawberries and tomatoes. It was impressive how much food we grew on that little pie-shaped corner of Tuscarora Road and my father was proud and happy.

Cherries, plums, and lots of fresh vegetables were a treat for our family, but our Victory Garden was out of place in a city where steel mills two miles away spewed soot, dust, and other particulate matter over everything. I can recall playing in the garden with a magnet—when I dragged it through the sandy soil, it picked up iron filings courtesy of Bethlehem Steel. I could draw out long streamers of iron bits that I would then fashion into all kinds of lacy configurations. It was fun, but it doesn't say much about the air quality in our neighborhood.

My Father Buys an Old Farm

As far back as I can remember, I felt a tug in my heart when my family spoke about "the country." It instilled in me a deep desire to own a piece of earth, if it is indeed possible to own nature. To me, country meant unspoiled meadows and forests and all the wonderful plant and animal life I would find there.

Then came a great moment in my young life. My father came into a small inheritance and used it to buy land in the country. He searched newspaper ads, consulted with realtors, and after looking at several abandoned farms on the outskirts of the city, he found his "dream farm"—24 acres located in North Java, about 30 miles from Buffalo. We wouldn't live on it, but we could visit often and he would grow things there.

To call these acres a farm is an exaggeration. About half the land was wooded and the rest was abandoned cow pasture that had been invaded by shrubs and wild apple trees. It was not good farmland anymore, but the wild berry bushes and apple trees were prime habitat for grouse and woodcock. Indeed, on spring evenings we would crouch quietly in the field to watch and listen to the male woodcock's mating ritual as he rose high into the night sky, then chirped as he settled back to earth.

It's hard to imagine that any farmer could ever have made a living there, but a collapsed farmhouse and a weathered shed for farm machinery gave evidence of past habitation. And the fields had once supported a few head of cattle, as indicated by the old strands of barbed wire that marked the border of their pasture. The rusting wire still hung loosely from sagging gray fence posts, the lower strands draped with curtains of brown grass.

The wooded portion of the property was dominated by sugar maples and beeches that would have provided firewood to heat the house, and fuel for the kitchen stove. The sugar maples might also have yielded maple syrup. A broken cement culvert lay in one of the stream beds, evidence that there had once been road access to these working woods. Some of the trees were large, and when I walked among them the city boy in me felt as if I were in an unspoiled wilderness.

There were actually two small streams on the property, one flowing through the open field and the other through the woods. They joined at a corner of the farm to form a respectable trout brook. I roamed these woods and built small dams in the brook, always dreaming of someday having a farm of my own.

Our neighbor operated a real farm, one of the last remaining dairies in the area. He approached my father to explain that the fence between us was in bad shape and that it was the responsibility of landowners to care for one half of a common fence. Since my father was better at preaching than fence making, they agreed that he would furnish the materials and the farmer would build the new fence. I still remember the farmer asking permission to cut some white ash on our boundary to use for posts, explaining that ash was preferable to other trees because it split easily.

When we first visited our new property, there was no place to stay, so my father bought a tent, which we set up in the pasture near the brook. We cooked our meals on a Coleman stove and at night lit the tent with a Coleman lantern. It was often cold and damp, but I was happy because I felt as if I was beginning to live my dream.

This place, which we called "the farm," became central to our lives. We tore down what was left of the old farmhouse and fixed the shed to serve as our "home" on the farm. Near this shed was a marshy area where willows grew, promising a source of water. We purchased a large ceramic tile, like those used for road culverts, dug a trough into the wet soil, and set the tile in place. I covered it with a wooden lid onto which I bolted a hand-levered water pump, and it produced the best water we had ever tasted. My father boasted about his good water and carried jugs of it back to our home in Buffalo. It sure tasted better than any of that chlorinated city stuff.

The former farmhouse left a gaping cellar hole lined with fieldstone walls. These I pulled apart and used to build my mother a rock garden, which even got a bird bath in later years. I liked the looks of the rock garden, but snakes loved to bask on the warm rocks, which disturbed my mother.

I dreamed of that farm day and night. It was not much to look at, but it was land and it grew things and it was a place to keep my bees. My one colony grew to ten, and I suddenly had more honey than I knew what to do with. Mother was a good salesperson, though, and managed to get rid of most of it—much of it to the church's parishioners.

I wanted nothing more than to live on our farm. It didn't happen while I was in high school, but when I went to college I figured out a way to spend my first summer there—I raised chickens.

My parents were enthusiastic about the idea, so again I collected scraps of lumber and this time built a chicken coop. It was about ten feet long and eight feet wide with a gabled roof, which I thought was quite attractive.

My parents bought thirty chicks around Easter and raised them in the cellar in Buffalo until I returned from college. From Easter to May those chicks went from the cute stage to scruffy, smelly birds, but I moved them to my chicken coop in North Java and there I spent the summer.

The first week was fine and I spent the days daydreaming. Then I began to get lonely. By the time my parents came to visit, I could hardly talk because my vocal cords weren't getting any exercise. Finally we sold the chickens to a real farmer, and I was freed to daydream for the rest of that summer, mostly about what agricultural enterprise I could try next.

The Cattle Boat

My high school years were dismal. I went to a public school in South Buffalo, but the strict moralist principal set rigid rules. Boys and girls were separated and not allowed to speak to one another in the hallways between classes. There was a boys' entrance at one end of the building and a girls' entrance at the other, with a stairwell for the boys at their end and another for the girls at their end. The school didn't sponsor dances, which didn't make any difference to me because I didn't know how to dance anyway.

I tried to find something of interest to participate in and decided on the school orchestra. First I took clarinet lessons but I wasn't very good. When the music director said he needed more trombones, I switched to the trombone, but I wasn't good at that either, a fact that was made embarrassingly clear at a concert in front of hundreds of students.

We had practiced for months and our conductor was proud of our progress. But when it was time for the trombone section to make a lot of noise, the slide shot off my instrument and slid under the piano. I scrambled to retrieve it and still can see the dismayed expression on the conductor's face as I crawled on the floor. The audience, however, did not react. You could hear a pin drop. That marked the end of my high school musical career.

The one bright spot of my high school years took place in biology class when my teacher, Jessie Hoffman, noted my interest in living things. Observing that I liked to draw, she asked if I could illustrate a book she was writing. She actually paid me to do a number of special line drawings, but I never saw the book and, to this day, I'm not sure she was really writing one. I did, however, enjoy doing the drawings for her and was grateful for her encouragement.

Basically, I disliked school—it was too confining—and I just wanted to get out as soon as possible. When I learned that after the first semester of senior year I could take the required exams for my high school diploma and graduate early I jumped at the opportunity. Somehow I managed to squeak through all the tests and escape from my misery. But it was now only January, the middle of the school year, and I hadn't thought about what I'd do next.

It was 1946 and from my parents, I learned that some church groups were shipping heifers to Europe to rebuild herds destroyed in World War II. This Heifers for Europe Project needed cattle tenders, so I applied and, after a month of waiting, I got a call from Heifer headquarters telling me that I should travel to Newport News, Virginia, to be assigned to a cattle ship. Off I went by myself on my first adventure away from home.

At Newport News I was given seaman's papers and now, at age 16, I was ready to sail to Europe just one year after World War II ended. Before I boarded the assigned ship, I can remember standing on the dock watching a black man operating a crane to load baskets of hay into the hold. He called to me and asked if I was sailing on the ship he was loading. When I told him proudly that I was, he said, "I wouldn't. It looks big now, but when you're out to sea, it will be nothing more than a match box."

With these words echoing in my ears, I climbed aboard, anticipating adventure ahead. My particular cattle ship was called the "Pass Christian Victory." It was a converted Victory ship, a cargo vessel that had been used to transport supplies to our armed forces during the war. To reach the cattle pens, I had to descend from the deck on a steel ladder, which I learned I was going to do on a regular basis for the next few weeks. I was assigned to take care of ten pens of Holstein heifers, feeding them and cleaning up after them on the long voyage to Gadyna, Poland, on the Baltic Sea.

The cattle crew of fifteen was largely made up of conscientious objectors who were working off their civilian service requirements. I found them a flaky lot, mostly smart but rather conceited, self-indulgent, and pampered. They groused about my being in the group because I was only sixteen, and I can still remember one of them saying that what bothered him most on the ship was "sixteen." For the most part, I ignored the snobs and even managed to make a few friends.

On the first day of our voyage, we left the port of Newport News early in the morning with our assigned load of cattle, about 100 heifers in all. We cattle tenders were in a jovial mood at breakfast and when the steward came for our breakfast orders, he asked how each of us would like our eggs. One rosy cheeked young man said he wanted his eggs poached. Within minutes an enraged cook burst into the mess hall yelling, "Poached? Who the hell do you think you are?"

By noon we were out of the sheltered harbor and onto the open sea. The ship began to dip and sway, up, down, up, down, and soon almost everyone was sick and couldn't work. Things went well for me, though. I was doing the work of two cattle tenders and was too busy to have time to be sick.

We had been at sea for two weeks when we had to sail out of our way to the south to avoid a severe storm. Cattle began to die as disease spread in the confined space of their pens, and the carcasses had to be hoisted out of the hold by a crane and dumped overboard. We must have lost a dozen or so.

Finally we were in the English Channel. We passed the Straits of Dover where I saw the famous white cliffs, and then we reached Denmark, where we sailed through the Kiel Canal connecting the North Sea to the Baltic. I remember blond children lining the edge of the canal calling out for fruit. We had crates of oranges on board and we tossed them like snowballs to the happy kids. They were clean looking and well-behaved, and they cheered and waved to us.

When we got to the Baltic Sea, we had to slow our speed because the waters were still mined from the war. Buoys had been placed along a mine-cleared channel, and the ship would go from buoy to buoy, slowly passing each one and then speeding to the next. It was a long, slow trip from the Kiel Canal to Gadyna. When we finally reached our port, I was shocked to see the extent of bombed out buildings. The streets were still full of rubble and trash. Everywhere men and boys were selling wares, ranging from dishes to pistols. The local currency was cigarettes, not the worthless Polish zlotys. I still don't understand the value of cigarettes for trade, but everyone on the cattle boat could buy cartons of cigarettes from the commissary, so I purchased them like the rest and used them to buy several dainty teacups and saucers for my mother and binoculars for my father. Although I managed to buy nice gifts for my parents, it was pitiful to see the general poverty and misery left by the war.

Poland was then occupied by Russia, and Russian solders, some about my age, were stationed on our cattle boat to prevent looting. They were friendly and we tried to speak to each other in broken German. Although they guarded the ship, they were sympathetic to the hungry Poles and let them scavenge from the ship's garbage cans, which were always full because the ship's cook made twice as much of everything as we needed. I was appalled to see trays of uneaten pork chops and steaks thrown overboard.

We had been in port for two days when we were told the mayor of Gadyna wanted to take us to lunch. We took a small bus to a café on the outskirts of the city where we were wined and dined. The vodka flowed like water, and the mayor gave a long, flowery speech, at times emotional, expressing his gratitude for the cattle we brought to help restore the farms destroyed by the war. We were proud of our mission.

When the ship was ready for the return trip home, we left the dock and anchored in open water where the officers made an inspection to be sure that everything was secure. They found three stowaways hidden in one of the large ventilation ducts—a sorry lot who possessed only several loaves of bread and a jug of water for provisions. The captain called the harbor police who took them away, and I learned later from some of the other cattle tenders that he was sad to do it because he knew they would be treated harshly.

Our trip back was the reverse of the trip coming. We cleared the minefields and then the Kiel Canal, this time with no children to greet us as we went through late in the day. Our sail back across the Atlantic was uneventful with no cattle to tend to and no storms encountered. I spent a lot of time reading, playing cards, and sleeping. When we finally reached port in Virginia, I gathered my belongings and started to board an overnight ferry that would take me to Newport News. Just as I was leaving the dock, one of the other cattle tenders came to me with a small, fuzzy white puppy, saying it had been given to him in Poland but he couldn't keep it. The puppy was playful and awfully cute, and I couldn't say no. The puppy's name was Chopak, which in English means "Bozo" or something like that.

There were staterooms on the ferry, but I didn't have the money for one, so I didn't know what I would do with Chopak when it came time for me to sleep. Two teenage girls I happened to meet did have a stateroom and they conveniently fell in love with the puppy, so when they asked if they could keep him overnight, I was delighted. It must have been quite an experience for Chopak because, when they gave him back to me the next morning, he was smeared with lipstick.

When I returned to Buffalo, several churches that sponsored the Heifers for Europe Project immediately got in touch to hear a firsthand report from someone who had actually delivered some heifers. I'm not sure how good a public speaker I was, never having had to stand in front of a large audience before, but I tried hard and enjoyed some success.

Looking back, I see my trip to Poland as a great educational adventure. I learned a lot more about the effects of war and poverty than I ever could have learned in a classroom. The best part of the experience was knowing I had played a small role in bringing heifers to farms to help rebuild a war-torn country. The Poles were deeply grateful. My tales of the Heifers for Europe Project, which did, in fact, involve considerable risk, later amused my wife, who couldn't understand why my parents—who were reluctant to let me go to high school parties—allowed me to sail through minefields and spend a week in a war-torn port where I fell asleep to the sound of celebrating Poles firing off guns every night.

College Years

If it hadn't been for my mother, I would never have gone to college. She knew my high school years had been miserable. I had made it more than clear to her that I felt the time I spent at Buffalo's South Park High School was more like being in prison than in a place of learning. She kept assuring me that college life would be different and something to look forward to, but I was not convinced and made no attempt to look at colleges I might like to attend. Taking the initiative while I was off on the cattle boat, my mother just went ahead and enrolled me at Heidelberg College in Tiffin, Ohio, where my older brother had gone several years before. She filled out all the admission forms, said "Sign here," and the next thing I knew I was off to college.

Heidelberg was a church-affiliated school founded by evangelical and reformed denominations that eventually became the United Church of Christ. My father was a United Church of Christ minister, and the college gave ministers a tuition break for their children, which was another reason for me to go there. The school enrolled about eight hundred students and had a small but dedicated faculty who were overworked and underpaid. The college was also trying hard to hold onto traditional church values that were changing with the times, and I can still recall the painful chapel sessions at ten o'clock every Tuesday and Thursday mornings, when ministers and upstanding members of the community would preach to a captive audience for one awful hour. A senior honors student sat in the back of the chapel and took attendance, which was obligatory. Meanwhile, I sat in the balcony snoozing or daydreaming of our farm in North Java, where I planned to live, keep my bees, and raise chickens.

The school had dorms for women but none for men. We had to find rooms in town. Because of a shortage of rooms when I arrived, I was assigned to the president's house along with three other men who were war veterans and a lot older than I. We were housed in two bedrooms; I shared a bed with a six-foot-six basketball player who had a girlfriend and, fortunately for me, did not spend much time in our room. We students were all noisy and messy and stayed up late at night smoking cigars and playing pinochle. At the end of the semester, the president's wife asked us to leave.

I took a room in a rundown but tidy house that stood next to the railroad tracks that ran along one side of the campus. Mrs. Doncyson was our housemother, a kindly widow who listened to soap operas on the radio all day and then later spoke about them as if they were real and a part of her life. There were three other roomers in the house, one a sports fanatic who could talk about nothing else, and two obnoxious theological students who could not hide their conceit.

I enjoyed the freedom of college life and took too much advantage of it. Having felt caged in that miserable Buffalo high school, I was exuberant in my new unstructured environment. I played hard during my first year and barely passed my courses. It was clear I was not going to be a distinguished scholar, but I did excel in playing pinochle, drinking beer, and smoking cigars.

To ensure that I would enjoy plenty of that kind of fun during my college years, I joined the Aptonalton Literary Society, a misnomer for the biggest bunch of beer drinkers on campus. There were two other "societies" at Heidelberg, one for the athletes and jocks and the other for pretheological students and the more intellectual types who were the spiritual leaders on campus. The Aptonalton Literary Society, known as the Aps, was assigned to a large graceless room in the main administration building where we held weekly meetings. The hall would fill with cigar smoke, but there were always two gas masks hanging from the wall for those with weak eyes and lungs.

Nothing much of importance took place during our smoky meetings in what was called the Aptonalton Literary Hall, but we enjoyed a lot of joking and laughter. About the only events of significance we had to organize were the annual prom and an evening we spent serenading the girls at their dorms. The singing was preceded by uncorking a well-hidden barrel of beer. Then we went from dorm to dorm, where the girls sat in the windows and cheered, which encouraged our brave singers to drink more beer and sing louder. We thought we sounded pretty good, but I'm not sure what the girls thought.

Not having had any dating experience in high school, I was shy and uneasy with girls. After several awkward dates during my first year at Heidelberg, I was about to give up, but in my sophomore year, I met Marie. Several years later, she became my wife.

Marie was a freshman, a music student majoring in piano and organ. Her father was a minister, as was mine, and we belonged to similar denominations. Marie was a gifted musician and was amused at my struggles learning to play the piano. We often practiced in the evenings in the same music building and, when we finished, I would walk her back to her dorm.

My brother, Stu, although he had already graduated, decided he would spend another year at Heidelberg and take some courses he had missed earlier. Stu had a wonderful tenor voice and sang in choral groups. The producer of a local radio station heard him and said, "You have a voice that must be heard!" So every Friday at 6:45 p.m. the station opened with a silky voice saying, "You will now hear the golden voice of Stuart Vogelmann." Marie was his accompanist, so she would play a few chords, and Stu would begin to sing. My job was to sit next to Marie and turn pages.

To be a good page turner, you have to follow along with the music so you can flip the page without interrupting the accompanist. When I was slow, Marie would nod her head to prompt me, "Now." Once I fell several stanzas behind. Marie shook her head harder and harder until I finally grabbed the page, but I pulled the whole book onto the keyboard. Brother Stu sang on and Marie successfully faked the accompaniment. Somehow we managed to stay friends.

Our radio show lasted only one semester, which I am sure was a relief to everyone. Stu liked to sing offbeat German lieder such as "Er ist tote"—or "He is dead"—which did not appeal to the local farm folk. But at least I got to know Marie, and she became my first and only girlfriend ever.

Dating in Tiffin, Ohio, was challenging. The town had one good restaurant located inside the Gibson Hotel. It was a clean but shabby room where pipes hung from the ceiling, but the cook made delicious oyster chowder, which Marie loved. We went there only on special occasions, however, since the meals were expensive, at least for a couple of students. Mostly we had coffee at Sally's Diner about two blocks from campus. Sally's had three tables set in front of a large plate glass window that looked out onto the street. During winter, the diner was drafty, but a cup of coffee cost only ten cents and it was a place for us to sit and talk.

I had known Marie for only a few weeks when I realized Valentine's Day was at hand and I should do something. I bought a box of chocolates and took it to her dorm. I rang the bell to her room, looking forward to seeing her, but her roommate, Ellie, came to the door to meet me instead. Disappointed, I pushed the box of chocolates into Ellie's hand, said, "Give it to Marie," and turned to walk away. But Ellie stopped me.

"No, you must give it to her in person." That was exactly what I wanted to do but didn't know how to make it happen. Then Marie appeared at the door and I got to deliver her box of chocolates.

My next present came on Marie's birthday several months later. I couldn't think of what to get her that would be special enough, so I went window-shopping at the stores lining Market Street in downtown Tiffin. Suddenly I spotted the perfect gift—a bright yellow dress with black leaves printed on it.

"Wow," I thought, "Marie would look great in that!" But when Marie opened the package on her birthday, she laughed awkwardly, obviously uneasy at receiving something so personal from someone she had known for only a couple of months. I think her mother was outright shocked, but Marie wore it anyhow, and all I can say is that she did look great in that bright yellow dress.

These first years at Heidelberg were not what I would call golden. I wandered from course to course without much direction. My grades upset my mother, who I think prayed I would do better. Unfortunately I was pitted against my brother who had been a straight-A student at Heidelberg and graduated magna cum laude. But he didn't drink beer or play pinochle, and I've always thought that was too bad. He spent most of his time studying.

I took all the science courses that Heidelberg offered, which included biology, botany and geology, but there were not many to choose from. Most were taught by two or three faculty members who had to stretch their knowledge to keep ahead of their students. One teacher, however, made a big difference in my college life. His name was Arthur McQuate, or Mac, as students called him. Mac was slender with a bony face that reminded me of Abraham Lincoln. He had a large nose, wore thick glasses, and had a deep raspy voice, but he had a genuine love for nature and it resonated in his lectures, which spanned a broad range of subjects from botany to zoology, ornithology, bacteriology, and anything else that needed teaching.

Mac would lead bird walks from his home at six o'clock in the morning, and longer field trips on weekends. He was a gifted teacher and his enthusiasm and love for nature, especially botany, were contagious.

As my senior year wore on, my grades finally improved, and indeed the impossible happened—I earned straight A's. Mac asked what plans I had for after graduation, and I had to admit that I didn't have any. I hadn't thought about what I might do next. He suggested I go on to graduate school and recommended the University of Michigan where he had taken a master's degree and knew the faculty. I applied and was accepted into the Department of Botany at Michigan. All of a sudden, I was off to graduate school. That good advice from Mac paved the way for me to grow intellectually and was the beginning of what was to become a serious and satisfying career in science.

Graduate School

The University of Michigan was about as different from Heidelberg College as I could imagine, with as many students on campus as there were people in the whole town of Tiffin, Ohio. There were more faculty in the Botany Department than in all the sciences at Heidelberg, and each professor had a specialty that he or she taught in rigorous courses. It was all very exciting but a bit overwhelming for a student like me. The first thing I did was fail the entrance exam, but the Department chairman was kind and recognized that all the botany I knew was taught by one man. He said I should not be discouraged and assigned me to Dr. Pierre Dansereau, a new plant ecologist, who would serve as my advisor.

Although I entered graduate school in the Botany Department, I wondered if this was the right choice for me. Because I had experience raising pigeons, rabbits, chickens, and bees, I thought I might be better with wildlife than with plants. So, along with the required botany courses, I took a course in wildlife management. The students in this course were a casual lot who dressed in blue jeans and bright plaid shirts, but the difference between their studies and the courses in botany was enormous. The intellectual content of wildlife management was weak in those pre-Aldo Leopold days.

I could only handle the reproduction rates of so many deer, rabbits, pheasants, and the like without falling asleep. But the hook-and-bullet crowd enjoyed the course work along with the time they spent in the woods fishing and hunting, which was all they wanted to talk about. Wildlife management seemed to me to encourage a happy-go-lucky approach to life. Botany, on the other hand, seemed like a serious pursuit, and I felt that becoming a botanist would indeed be a noble profession.

So I stayed with botany, and Pierre Dansereau became my mentor for the next five years. He hailed from Montreal and was proud of his French heritage, pointing out that his name meant "little dancer." He seemed to believe the French were more intelligent than the rest of us, and for all I know, he may have been right. He enjoyed playing the part of a gracious Frenchman and often kissed the hands of women who almost swooned at his attention.

Pierre was a slender man with sharp, intense brown eyes, a hawk nose, and a carefully trimmed black mustache. He was bald on top but still had a rim of dark hair. The baldness seemed to bother him, so when his students saw a picture of him in earlier years with his thick mop intact, they assured him that he was better looking now, which pleased him.

Pierre wore a long white lab coat that swirled with his rapid movements and often caught on doorknobs and table edges. He was fast but not especially graceful. His voice was smooth, almost silky, and his words were carefully chosen. He was a master at describing people and events and, while he could be humorous, he was also sometimes blunt.

Pierre prided himself on being an intellectual and indeed he was. He had read the great classical works of literature and went to the ballet and theater. Moreover, he was never at a loss for words to let people know that his intellectual life extended beyond science. A devout Catholic, Pierre defended his religion, even in the face of science. When challenged, Pierre would draw himself up and say, "Religion stands by itself and you do not question." As graduate students, we were perplexed by this attitude from a man who was precise and exacting in his scientific research.

Pierre was married to a lovely woman named Francoise, whom he adored. The opposite of him in many ways, Francoise was an artist with a free, imaginative mind and uninhibited social behavior. She would often act like a happy cavorting child, reminding me of river otters who slide down steep banks for the pure joy of it. I recall one field trip that Pierre arranged for his graduate students to botanize in the Upper Peninsula of Michigan. He took along his colleague, Stanley Cain with his wife, Louise, me with Marie, who was by now my wife, and two other graduate students. At night we slept under the stars, and I can remember Francoise and Louise giggling late into the night. One night Francoise tried to get into her sleeping bag head first, embarrassing Pierre who felt this was not proper behavior in the presence of students.

During the day, Pierre and Stanley took us graduate students to bogs and old-age forests while Marie stayed behind with Francoise and Louise, joking with one another and making fun of the expedition. When we returned from one of our field trips, Marie told me that Francoise had gotten hold of *Gray's Manual of Botany*, a highly technical book that classifies plants and has complicated keys to identify them. She tried to pronounce the Latin names but found it impossible, so Louise and Marie joined in, and all three had great fun entertaining each other with their made-up pronunciations.

Pierre was a friendly man, but he criticized me for not reading more, especially the great works of literature. Once, when he was chastising me for my intellectual deficiencies, he asked if I had ever read *War and Peace*, and I quipped that I was waiting for it to be made into a movie. Those dark brown eyes flashed and he spun around in disgust, his white lab coat flying. I stood there hoping it would catch on the doorknob on his way out, but it didn't.

Pierre had his own interpretation of people and cultures, and he considered the French to be intellectuals, artists, and heavy thinkers. And how he enjoyed playing with words! Every morning he would gather students around his lab table to drink tea and discuss the latest news or scientific events. If you were there, you had better have a clear mind or you would be verbally destroyed. Indeed, whenever you were in Pierre's presence you had to be at your intellectual best. I struggled to meet his expectations, but I'm sure my efforts were never enough, and I've yet to read *War and Peace*.

The search for an ecological project to focus on for my doctoral work was difficult. I considered possibilities within various groups of plants like violets, toothworts, and goldenrods, but none of them seriously interested me. On our visits to the shores of Lake Michigan, however, we often explored the small marly beach pools that harbored a rich flora with an assortment of calcareous species such as the bird's-eye primrose. Indeed it was this particular primrose, *Primula mistassinica*, that finally caught my attention, became the subject of my doctoral dissertation, and consumed my research efforts for the rest of my graduate career.

Primula mistassinica is a highly variable species distributed throughout the northern hemisphere extending from the sub-arctic to the lakeshores and cliffs of northeastern United States. For my doctoral research I was to examine the ecology (relationship to its environment) and morphology (structures and their functions) of the species and understand its taxonomy (classification). The plant grows in a small rosette with a flower stalk about six inches tall. Typically it has a blue or purple tubular flower with a bright yellow center or eye. The leaves are sometimes covered with a whitish waxy powder but are often bare. Sometimes the leaves have a smooth margin and at other times they are toothed. Of particular interest to me were those specimens with white flowers found on wet north-facing cliffs around Lake Michigan and eastward to the Finger Lakes of central New York.

One summer I traveled to the Gaspé Peninsula on the St. Lawrence River with two botanists from the Montreal Botanical Gardens who collected seeds from native species for catalog distribution. Neither could drive a car so I was their chauffeur for ten days, driving them along the Gaspé coastline in the lumbering old Dodge my father had sold to me at a bargain price when I started traveling for my research. On that trip, I found a primrose named *Primula laurentiana* growing on the calcareous rocks and ledges bordering the Gulf of St. Lawrence. It seemed a lot like *Primula mistassinica* so I carefully collected live specimens to grow in the botanical garden back at the University of Michigan. I wanted to see exactly how these two primroses were related.

The head gardener at the University of Michigan, Walter Kleinschmidt, grew my specimens with loving care. Primroses require a cool, moist environment, so Kleinschmidt made cheesecloth tents to cover the plants, which he set on trays of water to maintain the right temperature and humidity. When I examined the chromosomes of the

Gaspé plants, I discovered several extra sets and confirmed that they were therefore different from my dissertation species.

I also took seeds from specimens loaned from other herbaria, germinated them, and added them to my greenhouse collection to give me a geographical representation from areas I couldn't visit. Under uniform growing conditions, I could separate genetic variations from those that were environmentally induced. In the end, my research demonstrated that *Primula mistassinica* was a single but highly variable species.

I enjoyed the collecting experience and learned a lot about plant ecology during this period. The title I chose for my dissertation was "A Biosystematic Study of *Primula mistassinica*," which sounds impressive, but looking back, I find it a rather undistinguished piece of science. My doctoral committee was kind enough to accept it, though, perhaps hoping I would do better in the future. I'm embarrassed to admit it, but later, when I was working with graduate students myself, I don't think I would have accepted my own dissertation from one of my doctoral students.

Marie

B ut I need to backtrack a little here, returning to the summer after my first year in graduate school at Michigan, and Marie.

Even after I graduated from Heidelberg, Marie remained my one and only girlfriend. The next June, when she graduated from Heidelberg, we were married—by *both* our fathers.

The wedding took place at Wenze's Church in Reading, Pennsylvania, where her father was the minister. We wanted just a simple family wedding, but her mother had other plans, and we ended up with a couple of hundred parishioners attending. Worse, *both* our fathers wanted to be the one to tie the knot, and there was plenty of tense discussion about how exactly it could be done. As it unfolded, Marie was in tears, and as I look back on our wedding day, I remember it as one of the most unpleasant days in my life.

Having survived the wedding, we spent our honeymoon at the University of Michigan's Biological Station on the shore of Douglas Lake in the northern part of the state. It was not the best place on earth to start married life, but I needed to take some field courses, and this was the place to be. Further, my major professor, Pierre Dansereau, was on the summer faculty there and needed me as his field assistant. When I was not doing field work, I was serving meals to faculty, who were a disgruntled lot and complained about my slow service. (I recommend the experience to all graduate students to help them learn the real character of their faculty heroes. Nothing brings out the beast better than slow service to a hungry professor.)

During the academic year Marie needed a job, and Pierre kindly hired her as his secretary. She was an excellent typist, fast and accurate.

She was also attractive, resourceful, had a good sense of humor, and got along well with Pierre. Indeed, he seemed to appreciate her and need her more than he needed me.

My second year as a graduate student, I was given a teaching fellowship and assigned to Elementary Botany laboratories. The responsibilities were minimal, consisting of taking attendance and making sure the microscopes and slides were in good order. But the introduction to the day's work required a ten-minute presentation to the class, and the thought of talking in front of twenty students terrified me. I had never done more than talk to my pigeons, rabbits, and chickens—plus a few kind church groups who truly wanted to hear about my experiences with the Heifers for Europe Project.

To overcome my fear of public speaking, I would go to the laboratory the evening before class and dress rehearse. I would stand, chalk in hand, in front of the empty blackboard and give my little presentation to the empty room. Marie finally joined me and, as my audience of one, would listen attentively, even though I doubt if she was at all interested in what I was talking about. The next day, hands sweating, I would present my carefully rehearsed speech to a sympathetic and polite group of lab students. It was a trying experience but a great education. I learned a lot and it helped me gain confidence, even paving the way for my teaching career at the University of Vermont.

Our next set of adventures involved doing the research for my dissertation. Once I decided on a topic, I needed to visit as many primrose sites as possible and Marie accompanied me on most of these trips. My father's old Dodge was comfortable and roomy, with plenty of space for a tent and camping gear as well as my collecting equipment. Marie was a good companion, and she helped me by taking field notes, collecting and pressing plants, and providing meals at the end of the day. Our firstborn son, Tom, came along during this period. Fortunately, my mother loved children and gladly cared for him when we went camping. We were often gone for two or three weeks at a time during the advanced stages of my research, but I never heard a complaint from my mother, who enjoyed being part of Tom's young life. Tom did well under the system, too, and eventually became a botanist himself.

A travel grant from the University of Michigan Graduate School provided funds that allowed me to search for primroses throughout most of their range. I was now a happy graduate student engaged in a focused research project that would take me to a number of very interesting places, but I needed a plan. I decided to use herbarium specimens, which were carefully documented, to determine the locations of where various primroses could be found, and I created a road map for our travels.

The longest trip took us out to the Colorado Rockies and Utah desert. I knew primroses flourished in the high wet meadows near Boulder, so our first stop was the herbarium at the University of Colorado, where I examined pressed specimens of *Primula incana* collected in the nearby mountains. As I sorted through the collection, I found one herbarium sheet with several large primroses artfully mounted with smaller specimens used to fill in the spaces. Looking closely, I noted the smaller plants were *Primula egalikcensis*, a species heretofore known to grow only in the Canadian arctic. It was the first record of the species in the United States and a great discovery for a young graduate student. Past plant collectors in Colorado, some of them very respected scientists, had apparently focused only on the large healthy looking plants and, as a result, missed the little primrose I was lucky enough to spot in a place explored by famous botanists for a hundred years.

Our most memorable stop on these excursions was in the desert near Moab, Utah, where the rugged landscape is both spectacular and forbidding—and sometimes taxing to the energy and patience of a budding botanist, not to mention his young wife. The topography there is characterized by red sandstone bluffs and box canyons. At the end of the canyons are high walls eroded at the base to form shallow caves that harbor an unusual flora. To reach the caves, I had to scramble up steep, sandy, rock-strewn slopes. I also had to take each step carefully to avoid stepping on the occasional basking rattlesnake. But when I reached a cave, I could stand in the cool shade of the overhanging rock ledge as if I were standing under a huge tree on a hot summer day.

The overhanging ledges and towering cliffs made me feel as if I were working in a giant amphitheater—my every footstep echoed from the canyon walls. At the back of the caves, I found a sandy rock face lined with water-porous bands where species that normally grow in cooler climates clung to the soft wet rock. A rare primrose, *Primula specuicola*, grows here along with species found in eastern deciduous forests such as maidenhair fern and Solomon's seal. I was amazed to find these familiar woodland species surviving in a desert where temperatures exceed 100 degrees Fahrenheit, but the caves offer shade and protect the dripping faces of the porous sandstone that provide the cool, moist microclimate these plants need.

Working in what felt like a huge geological arena gave me a new, more extended sense of time, with its companions: a constantly changing climate and relentless geological processes. As water seeps slowly from the canyon walls here, erosion carves out the shallow caves that shelter plants surviving from a time when the climate was cooler and wetter than it is now. Primroses cling to their fragile toehold on the seeps, but eventually the cave wall will be cut back to the point where the roof will collapse, wiping out the local flora. But elsewhere, erosion is cutting new caves in other box canyons to form new habitats where the seeds of the old primroses can still grow. These cycles take thousands of years, and my visit lasted only a microsecond on this scale of time.

By the end of that summer, Marie and I had traveled several thousand miles and collected hundreds of primroses. I felt as if primroses had truly become an important part of my life, as important even as my growing young family. Through it all, I learned a lot about both plant ecology and the personalities of other botanists who helped me in my research. Back in Ann Arbor, I settled down to watch my primroses grow and organize my travels into a serious doctoral dissertation. Our hunt for primroses in far-flung places provided a valuable understanding of field ecology and the forces that shape the distribution and evolution of plants—an education the classroom and laboratory could never have given me. It also provided Marie and me with wonderful experiences that still trigger fond memories.

Vermont 1955

My introduction to Vermont began in 1955, during my last year in graduate school, when Pierre Dansereau asked me what I was going to do after I finished my Ph.D. I had to confess once again that I hadn't given my future much thought because I was having such a good time doing what I was doing with my primroses. Pierre told me there was a position open in the Botany Department at the University of Vermont. Naive young scientist that I was, I asked, "Where's Vermont?" and Pierre made me look it up on a map of New England.

There it was, sandwiched between New York and New Hampshire. Even if my geography was about as bad as my reading habits, I followed Pierre's good advice and applied for the job. That spring I was invited for an interview. Getting to Vermont from Michigan was going to be a problem, but Pierre told me that he and Francoise would be driving to Montreal during spring vacation and I could ride with them. From there I could take a bus down to Burlington, Vermont. When the time came, I squeezed into the back seat of the Dansereaus' Volkswagen Beetle and off we went. It took two long days of driving to travel across southern Canada to Montreal, but at least the bus ride down to Burlington gave me some time to stretch my legs.

I had made arrangements to meet the chairman of the Botany Department at the bus station on the evening of my arrival. Emerging from the dingy station, I looked around to see a small park surrounded by numerous old brick buildings—my first view of Vermont. What I remember most is that I was freezing. It was March and the weather was still bitter cold. I waited—and waited some more. A few times I ducked back into the bus station to warm myself, but I got colder and colder as I continued to wait. Finally, a Ford station wagon with wooden side panels sped up to the curb, and a man in a heavy overcoat jumped out and dashed into the bus station. I wondered, "Could that be him?" He raced back out, ran to the station wagon, spoke to his wife inside, and finally looked back at me. God, I was cold. He finally approached me and asked my name.

"Hub Vogelmann," I said.

"OK, but you sure don't look like your picture. Hop into the car."

And off we went. He did a sharp u-turn and stopped in front of Vermont's finest hotel, which was directly across the street from the bus station. "See you in the morning," he said, and rushed off at a pace I later learned was Jim Marvin's trademark.

Jim eventually turned out to be one of my best friends, and I always enjoyed the time I spent with him. He had a warm personality and could get along with almost anybody, but more importantly, he had energy, vision, and the ability to make good things happen.

The next morning Jim met me at the hotel and took me to the University to meet the Botany Department faculty. They were friendly but somewhat awkward and reserved. I was the first possible addition to the department in ten years, and they didn't want to get stuck with a loser. After a morning of greetings and introductions, a group of them took me to lunch at the Old Board, a quaint restaurant not far from campus. There was Jim Marvin, with a Vermont sense of humor that I didn't understand at the time but grew to appreciate over the years. Fred Taylor was quiet, careful, and modest. Louise Raynor, the only woman in the department, was cheerful, upbeat, and tried to make this a light occasion. She pointed out that the younger members of the department were in their mid-40's, and she was the youngest at forty-four. I was only twenty-six, but they didn't look all that old to me.

Two members of the department didn't come to the lunch. One was Alex Gershoy, a distinguished man with white hair that made a curl over his forehead. He was in his late fifties and had made his botanical reputation with studies on the genetics of violets. It was brilliant work and I had heard about it long before my visit to Vermont. These days he did little research except to dabble in the genetics of bird's-foot trefoil. I learned later that he had been successful in developing a strain called Mansfield. Alex loved to talk, and once you were cornered, he was difficult to escape. He was close to being one of those rare true intellectuals I've learned to recognize over the years. By this time, though, he spent most of his time in the greenhouse smoking cigars and puttering around with pots of trefoil seedlings. I remember he kept a tennis racket in his office and enjoyed playing a game whenever he could.

The other faculty member who missed the lunch was plant pathologist Tom Sproston, a small man with a crooked smile. I always heard that pathologists were difficult people, so I tried hard to impress him with some unwarranted flattery about his research. It helped get me through an interview with him but he was never particularly friendly. In fact, after I was hired he didn't speak to me for a year. Later I learned that he had suggested a friend of his for my position and was disappointed that I had been hired instead.

Jim Marvin wanted me to meet the dean of the College of Agriculture, Joe Carrigan. Dean Carrigan was a friendly person, skilled in dealing with the state legislature, and because of that skill the college always had enough money to carry out good teaching and research programs. He had a kind heart and looked after his faculty. He looked me over and asked how old I was. I straightened up and confessed, "Twenty-six."

He turned to Jim and said, "I don't know. He looks pretty young to me." My heart sank. I had decided I really wanted this job.

After two long days, the interviews were done, and I returned to Ann Arbor to mull over the experience. I flew back on a DC-3, which sure beat the Dansereaus' Volkswagen Beetle. Years later I was to fly again on a DC-3 over the Andes Mountains in Colombia on a botanical expedition to collect medicinal plants. It was a great plane, but I remember looking out the window on the Colombia trip and noting the cowling over one engine was tied together with bailing wire.

But that's another story. First I had to get a job. The University of Vermont did hire me despite my youth—and wound up getting me for life.

Knob Lake

S ome of my graduate school experiences stayed with me long after I completed my Ph.D. The Botany Department at the University of Michigan was a busy place where renowned scholars presented weekly seminars. Some were brilliant lecturers, others dull, but they always sparked lively discussions about everything from evolution to photosynthesis. These were invigorating and stimulating sessions for us graduate students, and we were always careful to attend. The Department chair would look over the audience, mentally taking attendance, and we would all but shout "Present!" both to show our interest in botany and to insure the renewal of our fellowships for the next year.

I always sat in the back of the room because I feared I might be called on for a comment or a question and I'd say something stupid. But I listened and watched with keen interest as distinguished botanists spoke of their travels and findings. One man had just returned from botanizing in Alaska; another reported on finding rare plants in the Himalayas; yet another had explored the Amazon. The one who really captured my imagination, though, reported on what he called a new botanical frontier, a place in northern Labrador called Knob Lake. The name struck a responsive chord in me, conjuring up a vision of a cold northern place of high adventure. The Far North began to beckon.

In my first year at the University of Vermont, I taught elementary botany courses and began to look for research projects beyond the primroses that had earned me my Ph.D. Something about arctic environments continued to draw me and I always looked northward for a project. Indeed, after I got the University of Vermont's job offer, I received a telegram from the University of Alaska offering me a job that would pay half again as much as Vermont was paying. I anguished over which job to accept, but Pierre told me to go to Vermont, and I trusted his advice, so I wired Alaska to reject their offer. I was so conflicted, though, that right after I send the wire, I called Western Union to ask them to hold the telegram. But it was already too late—and thus ended that particular arctic fantasy, leaving me with only the fragments of boreal vegetation scattered on the tops of Vermont's highest mountains as prospects for future Arctic-Alpine research.

During my second year at UVM, I received a call from Pierre telling me about an opportunity to do fieldwork at McGill's Subarctic Research Station at Knob Lake. All the grad school images of that wild northern place flooded back into my mind. I said to Marie, "Let's go!" As usual, she was game to come along as my field assistant, and I applied for the summer fellowship. It required only that I do independent field studies and report my findings at the end of the summer, which seemed easy enough, so we looked forward to the whole experience as another grand botanical adventure.

In the middle of June, we heard that the ice on Knob Lake had melted, which meant the subarctic winter had ended and I could get started on my research. By now Marie and I had two sons—Tom, who was five, and Jim, who wasn't a year old yet—and my mother, bless her, was willing to take care of both of them while we were away. As soon as we had gotten the boys settled, we flew to Quebec City and from there to a grassy air strip at Knob Lake. Looking out the plane window, I saw a vast carpet of white lichens and small scattered spruces interrupted by hundreds of lakes and bogs. This was where I wanted to be—a new and more exciting botanical world than I had ever seen before—or at least so I thought.

The first thing I learned was that, since my graduate school days, Knob Lake had lost its original name. The town was now called Schefferville, named for a local priest, and it was a hastily built place crisscrossed by muddy roads, nothing like my romantic vision of it when I was still a student. Rich iron ore deposits lay on the surface of the land where they were scraped up by huge dozers and loaded into waiting trucks that were in turn loaded onto rail cars. From Schefferville, the ore was taken by the newly constructed railroad to Seven Islands on the north shore of the Gulf of St. Lawrence to be shipped out to other ports. I recall miners complaining about digging in permafrost in weather so cold it froze the ore onto the machinery and the freight cars. A dreary looking town, Schefferville was indeed an inhospitable place for human beings and plants alike.

I found the countryside around the town raw and barren. It looked as if a glacier had just melted there, and pollen studies on nearby bogs indicated that the ice had left this area only three thousand years ago, almost yesterday in geological terms. In Schefferville, soil was referred to as "an anticipated geological event"—something that hadn't arrived yet. In some places permafrost penetrated to a depth of a hundred feet or more, and on exposed ground frost action sometimes sorted stones into polygonal patterns. Small, widely spaced spruces and clumps of shrubby birches provided little relief to this lichen-covered landscape, and these trees grew as slowly as did everything else. I measured a two-foot-tall spruce and learned that it was seventeen years old. Here I was surrounded by classic taiga—a northern vegetation type that stretches in a broad belt from Labrador to Alaska, covering thousands of square miles, an area larger than all of New England and New York combined—but I was already feeling less romantic about this cold and bleak environment.

The Subarctic Research Station occupied a small frame building near the air strip, and Marie and I were assigned to two small rooms with a bed and kitchen. Now, without direction, I was to begin my fieldwork, whatever that would be. Much of the taiga surrounding Schefferville had been burned ten years earlier. It seemed unlikely that fires could burn through the scattered spruces, but I learned that when the foot-thick lichen mat dries, it will burn furiously. With nothing to stop the fire, it can spread over thousands of acres. I decided to look at the succession of plants that come back after a fire, starting with the mosses and lichens that were already slowly spreading over the burned terrain.

I found five species of lichens, most in the genus *Cladonia*. One white puffy species, *Cladonia alpestris*, grew in clumps that looked like clustered snowballs. Walking on a dry lichen mat leaves footprints that can last ten years or more because lichens grow so slowly—no more than a quarter of an inch a year. Usually the mat is kept wet with constant drizzle and cloudy days, but when a period of dry weather arrives the mat dries out and breaks into polygons that pull apart, creating narrow openings to the soil below. These cracks form seedbeds for invading plants such as birches, black crowberry, and mountain cranberry.

For part of my research, Marie and I stretched a tape along the ground and carefully recorded the changes of plant species along a transition from raw soil to invading mosses and lichens. Was it fun? No. The black flies were unbearable. In the morning, before departing to the field, we would pull on long pants and long-sleeved shirts. Then we tied string or rubber bands around the cuffs of both to prevent black flies from getting at us, but it was hopeless. They always found an opening to crawl through and chew holes in our skin. The blood spots on our shirts were evidence that black flies had gotten to us.

We found out that biting insects are attracted to dark clothing, especially blues. Marie took a photo of dozens of mosquitoes congregating on the back of my blue cotton shirt, but it wasn't the mosquitoes that were bothering me—it was the cloud of black flies that buzzed around my face while she took the photo. I have heard of downed pilots stranded in the subarctic going crazy from the black flies, and I can believe it. We learned that local Indians sometimes ignited the dry lichen mat and sat in the smoke to escape the flies. Some of these untended fires spread, burning without control and contributing to the destruction of the subarctic forests.

The only way for me to travel from Schefferville to other areas and regions was by plane, which was difficult. I would sit at the airfield waiting for a ride like a hitchhiker. I was lucky that the pilots who ferried in supplies to ground survey crews were friendly and helpful. I often squeezed into a jump seat or sat in a cargo hold, but I did get to explore new places far from Schefferville and even managed to visit the high arctic at the tip of the Ungava Peninsula.

The best part of that summer was that I love to fish and the subarctic is a fisherman's paradise. Virgin streams and lakes teem with hungry trout that pounce on any lure thrown in their direction. They would fight among themselves to be the first to grab my bait, which could be a bent spoon or a tin can lid. It was great sport and provided Marie and me with good food at the end of the day as we tended to our black fly bites.

By summer's end, I had learned to recognize many species of lichen and moss as well as much of the vascular flora of the subarctic. I established a plant collection that is now housed in the Pringle Herbarium at the University of Vermont, and I wrote a short account of my findings that appeared in the Subarctic Research Station's annual report. I don't have much else to show for that summer except for a bit of my continuing botanical education, plus a less romantic view of the vast northern frontier that is still largely unexplored—as it will likely remain until someone figures out how to deal with black flies.

When I got home, I felt more comfortable with my decision to take the job at the University of Vermont. Fragments of arctic-alpine vegetation on Vermont's tallest mountains offered me plenty of opportunities for future research, but before I could focus all my attention on Vermont, other opportunities would arise.

Colombia

In the mid-1960s, Dr. Richard Schultes, curator of the herbarium at Harvard, was organizing an expedition to South America to collect medicinal plants. The man who was supposed to lead the group had backed out at the last minute, and Dr. Schultes invited me to take his place. At the time, I was busy teaching a summer school course, but the course would end just in time for me to make the trip, so I said I'd go.

The expedition was to leave in just two weeks, and it occurred to me that I should try to learn some Spanish before I left, so I bought a set of records guaranteed to teach Spanish in a few easy lessons. Each morning before my summer school class began, I listened to the records and practiced, but I soon realized that whatever Spanish I might learn during those frantic two weeks wasn't going to be enough.

The plan was for me to fly to Bogota, Colombia, and meet up with two graduate students from Harvard. The three of us, with me in charge, would work as a team collecting specimens for the herbarium. I remember flying into Bogota and looking out the window of the plane at the mountains and patterned landscape below.

I was excited, but when we landed I found myself pushing through crowds of Spanish-speaking people, feeling totally confused and lost. I tried out my new Spanish—all those handy expressions my language records promised would work—but no one could understand me. Or maybe they were bewildered by what I was actually saying. They just looked at me in amazement as I announced, "I am hungry," "I am thirsty," and "I need to go to the bathroom."

Somehow I managed to get out of the airport and find a taxi that took me to the pension where I was to meet the Harvard students I would lead into the wilds of Colombia. The next day the three of us flew in a rickety DC-3 to Pasto, a town near the border of Ecuador. We set up our base of operations in Pasto, where a small college had designated a staff person to help us organize our forays into the backcountry to collect medicinal plants.

Local Colombian workers accompanied us on each trip, and I had to give them detailed directions about our collecting procedures. Not one of them spoke a word of English and, as the days passed, my Spanish pocket dictionary became more and more ragged. By the end of each day, I collapsed into bed immediately after dinner.

Far too soon, it was dawn again, and we were off to the field for another day of botanizing in Spanish. Every day I listened to their our workers' Spanish, struggling to understand and learn from it. I also worked hard to make my own Spanish understood—all day, listening and speaking, listening and speaking, until my head ached. I knew I was in trouble when I began to dream in Spanish and even the people in my dreams couldn't understand me.

The memory of one incident remains vivid. I was standing beside the road late one afternoon waiting for our truck to pick me up. A woman with two children stood nearby, obviously aware that I was a foreigner. I thought this might be a good opportunity to practice being social in Spanish. I tried to look friendly and said, "Buenos dias," which I knew meant "Good day," but to native Spanish speakers it indicates "Good morning." Much to the woman's embarrassment, the children started giggling. She shushed them but not before I realized that even children found my Spanish laughable.

Despite the language challenges, I learned volumes while leading the expedition. At first we focused on plants found in the countryside within a day's drive around Pasto. At a variety of sites, we picked and separated leaves, bark, roots, flowers, and fruits and put the whole batch of plant materials into burlap bags. The plant parts were dried at the lab in Pasto and sent by air to the United States for chemical analysis.

One of our forays led to Vulcan Galeras, a 12,000-foot volcanic mountain that dominates the Pasto valley. One of our young Colombian workers remembered an eruption and said it was like an atomic explosion. I read that it had erupted in 1993, and this time several geologists working near the rim of the crater were killed. The reporter offered a terrifying account of how they had tried to escape but were trapped and fell into the crater. The volcano continues to be active today, possibly the most active on the South American continent.

I had collected some low-growing cushion plants at the rim of the very crater that had claimed the lives of the scientists. At the time I collected the specimens, I had been surprised to find they looked like some arctic species I saw on a brief visit to the tip of the Ungava Peninsula during the summer at Knob Lake. This area close to the volcano's crater had an eerie feel. When I looked down into the crater itself, I felt weak. I could see sulfur fumes rising from the crater floor, and clouds drifting upward. A strong wind tugged at my body, and I had to be careful it didn't blow me over the edge. Our workers complained about the bitter cold—and it was cold, even by Vermont standards. Our hands numbed as we worked, and the low oxygen at this elevation made it difficult to breathe.

Just below the volcano's summit was a subalpine zone where we encountered the strangest vegetation I have ever seen. The plateau region is called a *paramo* and it included some of the most distinctive plants in the world. A ten-foot-tall composite called *Espelitia* dominated the area. The plants were pale gray, widely spaced, and looked like giant sagebrush growing in a desert. They had thick felt-like leaves that resembled the leaves of mullein but much larger. When we tried to cut through the plants with our machetes, it was like hacking away at soft pillows. An equally strange tree form of giant *Lobelia* grew there, and I later learned that the vegetation in this part of the Andes is like that found in the Mountains of the Moon region of central Africa.

The whole scene was spectacular. We could see for miles from atop the volcano, and in the valley below, the cultivated lands lay like a giant jigsaw puzzle of greens and browns.

After we exhausted the collecting sites around Pasto, we learned of an excellent place to find medicinal plants in the Putumayo River valley. The Putumayo is a tributary of the Upper Amazon, and the site we wanted to visit was a two-day drive from Pasto, an area so remote that few botanists had ever visited it. We decided to head for Mocoa, a small town bordering the river. A German settler who lived on the way arranged to meet us there.

This man, George Feuerbringer, was a strong-minded and energetic retiree who loved Colombia and enjoyed his isolated lifestyle. The drive over the mountains on our way to meet him was a botanical treat. The tropical forest along the road was green and lush. Waterfalls spilled onto the road from the steep slopes above. The trees were huge, their thick limbs spreading horizontally and festooned with Spanish moss, bromeliads, and orchids. We were passing through a truly virgin tropical forest so inaccessible that it had never been cut.

We drove along a winding road slowed by mud slides, which were common. It was a long, grueling trip and it was dark and raining by the time we reached the spot where we met George. We gathered our gear from the truck and slung some of it onto a horse that George had thoughtfully brought along. But tired as we were, we had to walk two miles to George's house over trails that were sticky and slippery with tropical red clay soaked by the rain.

After a quick dinner, we prepared for bed. Fred Olday, one of the Harvard graduate students, left for bed first and I remained behind to visit with George. After a while I went to the room I would share with Fred and found him still wide awake.

"Look at what I just found in my shoe," he said, and held up a huge tarantula that he had beaten to death with his other shoe. It was the biggest spider I had ever seen. When he threw it out of the room, it hit the floor with a thud.

The next morning I had a chance to look more closely at George's house. It was large and airy with an open porch that wrapped around two sides. George explained how all the timbers were sawed by hand. Logs were placed over a deep pit in which one man stood while another man stood above. Together they pushed and pulled a two-man saw back and forth, painstakingly cutting out planks and timbers.

George proudly told us that before he came to Colombia, he had hired a man to find the best place to retire, and that was where he chose to settle. His home was in the middle of a magnificent jungle, but he had cleared enough space around his house so he could look out over the valley. The only civilization visible from his land was an Indian village below with its small grass huts showing through the forest.

After breakfast I went onto the porch with a pan of water and a mirror to shave. I propped the mirror against a post, lathered my face, and lifted my razor—at which point a stone whizzed past my head and bounced off the nearby wall. Then came another, this one closer. I jumped back and searched for whoever was throwing stones at me. There at the end of the porch was a Capuchin monkey in a pink dress watching me and getting ready to throw another stone. It looked downright human. I soon learned it was a male named Ramon and I was told he had the mentality of a three-year-old child.

Ramon was kept on a leash along with a brown mongrel dog that he would hug around the neck, clinging to the dog as a small child might. The monkey had a pail of water and some tin cookie cutters to play with, and he would pour water onto the ground to make mud pies that he shaped with the cookie cutters. That first morning, he continued to eye me as if he intended to throw another stone. I don't think he liked strangers.

Besides the monkey and the dog, George also had a parrot that sat on a perch at the edge of the porch near where Ramon had stood to throw the stones at me. The parrot spoke Spanish, which left me out of any possible conversations. The handsome bird was bright green and sat in a stiff upright position. I couldn't resist turning him upside down to see what he would do, but he just stayed as he was, clinging proudly to his bar until I turned him right side up again.

George's life was like something out of the 1800s. He lived with an Indian woman who was part slave and part wife, as far as I could tell. She, with a young girl helper, prepared our meals but were never allowed to eat with us. Men were supposed to be waited on, and it would be a breach of etiquette for women to eat with us. George did seem to appreciate his companion, however, and I think he loved her. They had a daughter, who at that time was in Russia studying to be a doctor. George was proud of her. Although he remained much the patrón in his marriage, he was a thoughtful and resourceful father.

Many unfamiliar plants grew in the tropical forest around George's house that were difficult for us to identify. In the evening we would press specimens to be identified later in the herbarium at Harvard. Because the harvested plants would mold quickly in the hot, humid air we had to prepare them by first bathing them in a pan of formaldehyde and then pressing them between newspapers. The specimens turned black but they didn't rot. It was a smelly, unpleasant chore, and the formaldehyde odor was difficult to get off our hands when we were ready for bed.

To identify unknown plants, you have to collect both flowers and fruits, the most critical parts needed to make a determination. Thousands of species grow in the tropics but few plant keys exist to help identify them, so we needed every plant part we could find in hopes that, when we got back home, we could figure out what we had. Fortunately, our workers, some of whom liked to show off their talents, were as skilled as monkeys climbing the trees, and they gathered flowers and fruits that were far out of reach from the ground.

On one occasion, we came upon a tree on the bank of a small stream. It looked like a good candidate for our collection, but the flowers and fruits grew high in the crown. One of our workers eagerly started up the trunk, but part way up he suddenly let go and dropped to the ground. "Ants," he said and refused to climb again. The workers told us horror stories about swarms of ants that could bite you and make you blind and said they knew of dogs and monkeys that were so afflicted.

Looking up into the canopy, I could see the large, brown, elongated mass that was the home of the ants, and it was indeed an impressive colony with insects running in all directions. We decided to cut the tree down with our machetes to collect the flowers and fruits. After it crashed to the ground, I pushed into the foliage at the crown and was amazed to find out we had cut down what looked like a tomato tree—a 70-foot-tall tomato tree!

It had yellow tomato-like flowers and the green tomato-like fruit just like those growing on the plants in my garden back home. The tree was obviously a member of the Solanaceae, the potato/tomato family. The tropics are full of surprises.

George arranged for us to travel to Mocoa to meet a settler who lived on the Putumayo River. It was a long dangerous ride over more mountains, on a narrow muddy road barely carved into the steep slopes. Sometimes I rode in the open cargo space to catch a breeze, but looking over the edge of the road into the deep valley below unsettled me. One of the workers told me it was best not to look.

The air in Mocoa was hot and humid and we found it hard to breathe. This riverside town looked amazingly like a scene from an old western movie with a muddy street lined by wooden hitching posts where horses were tied. Ours was the only vehicle, and we were an instant attraction. It must have been a long time since the natives had seen anyone from outside the region.

Out of a shabby building stepped a short man in an olive drab uniform with a pistol strapped to his waist. Suddenly we weren't in an old movie anymore. The man had a black mustache, small dark eyes, and a harsh look on his face. He looked like the sort of a person who could shoot you without batting an eye. George knew him and said we should be careful; he was the law in Mocoa.

We parked near the river and were greeted by a tall, slender man with a smile on his face—a relief after the local lawman. This was obviously a good friend of George's. We loaded our gear into his dugout canoe and took off up the river. A Johnson motor looked out of place hitched to the back of the dugout, but we didn't care as long as it worked. After an hour, we reached our host's house, which was a rustic, thatch-roofed structure perched on a high bank above the river. It made George's house look like a castle. Pigs and chickens shared the house with the family, and eventually with us, as we did our best to get to sleep on the floor.

George's friend was a poor local, but he tried to make us comfortable. His biggest worry was finding enough food for us to eat. When he caught a large catfish in the river, it supplied us for a couple of days. I gave him a traveler's check for ten dollars when we left, for which he was grateful. It likely amounted to a month's wages, and George thanked me for the gesture.

On our trip back to Pasto, the other Harvard graduate student, Doel Suharto, an Indonesian, took sick. He spent most of the day lying in the back of the truck, sitting up only to vomit over the side. By evening, he was so weak he could barely move. Only a few miles from

Pasto where there would be a hospital, we came to a mud slide that blocked the road. There was nothing to do but find a place to stay until the road could be cleared, which would take a day or two.

We located a small inn and put poor Doel to bed. He had a dangerously high fever, and I was afraid he would not last the first night. But hot soup and rest restored some of his strength. Eventually we got him to Pasto, where he was put on a plane back to the United States for hospital care. I learned later that it was two months before he was well again.

Looking back, remembering scenes from Mocoa still makes me wistful for a simple, unhurried life. It was a timeless world with few amenities, no electricity, only candles to light the evening. The only sounds were barking dogs, guitars, and singing—and there was always the smell of wood smoke in the air.

Mexico

After collecting medicinal plants in Colombia, I figured I was done with Spanish. But I soon learned that I would to have to wrestle with it again when an opportunity arose to pursue research in the cloud forests of Mexico.

These remarkable forests are located on the slopes of the Sierra Madre Mountains in eastern Mexico, and they were rapidly disappearing as Mexican peasants cleared them for agriculture. In 1966 I applied to the National Science Foundation for a grant to study the cloud forests before they were gone altogether. To my surprise and delight I was awarded the grant, which allowed me and my family to spend a whole academic year at the University of Mexico.

When the time came, I packed the family and a supply of clothing and essentials into our Volkswagen Microbus and set off for Mexico City. Driving with three young boys—Tom was now fourteen, Jim was ten, and our third son, Andy, was four—from Vermont to Mexico City was no small task, but the microbus gave the boys plenty of room to read and play during the five-day trip.

When we arrived in Mexico City and started looking for housing, Marie and I realized we would not find suitable accommodations in the city. A house the size our family needed would be too expensive in the good neighborhoods, and we wouldn't be comfortable in the run-down areas. Just when we were feeling desperate, I heard we might find reasonable housing in the town of Cuernavaca about fifty miles south of Mexico City.

In Cuernavaca I checked the family into a tacky motel where everything was painted a gaudy yellow in honor of its name, *Los Canarios,* and took off on my own, determined to find a decent place to live.

Finally, I found a beautiful house with a garden, a swimming pool, and a big black iron gate guarding the grounds. It was on the outskirts of town and a bit more expensive than I had planned for, but I rationalized that it came with a maid and gardener who would be helpful to us as we figured out how to live in Mexico. The family was delighted to leave *Los Canarios* and move into such luxury.

My sponsor at the University of Mexico was Arturo Gomez-Pompa, an energetic botanist with lots of ambition. Shortly after my arrival, I was working in the herbarium with Arturo when a friendly man approached. He was the dean and had come to welcome me to the University. After a few sentences in English, he switched to Spanish, and I was in trouble again.

I listened as intently as I could, trying to grasp what he was saying, but the words were coming too fast. To be polite, I kept saying "si" to everything he said. That was one word I had learned to say perfectly and without an accent.

"Si. Si. Si," I said, and got to feeling pretty good about the nice conversation we were having. Finally, he grabbed my hand, shook it, and left.

Arturo looked pale. "Why did you say you'd do that?" he asked.

I asked him what I had said I would do. He told me I had just agreed to give a lecture—in Spanish—to the Mexican Academy of Science. I was horrified, but I had made the commitment, so when they asked me for a topic, I said I would lecture on the ecology of the arctic. My trip to the tip of the Ungava Peninsula during the summer we spent at Knob Lake was still fresh in my mind, and I figured the Mexicans might not know much about that part of the world. I hoped they wouldn't and would find what I had to say interesting enough to forgive my Spanish.

I had several weeks to prepare and I used all of the time available. I wrote out every word and practiced what I had written on our maid, Leonora. She was patient and listened politely to everything I had to say about the subarctic, but I don't think she was the least bit interested in the subject.

When the day for my lecture finally arrived, I was nervous and couldn't believe I had gotten myself into this predicament. After

Arturo's flowery introduction, I took the podium and looked out over the audience. At least a hundred people stared back at me, all with dark skin, black hair, and all of whom spoke another language. At that moment, I felt disoriented and unsure what I was supposed to say. Then I remembered where I was and all the phrases I'd practiced with Leonora and somehow managed to get through the lecture. The audience was kind and asked me simple questions. I don't know what they learned about the arctic, but it may have been even less than my long suffering maid.

There were so many embarrassing moments in my efforts to use Spanish that it's hard to remember them all. Once I was driving our Volkswagen bus in Mexico City when the engine began to skip. It was obvious that the points should be replaced, so I drove to a nearby garage. The mechanic came out to greet me and asked what I needed and I realized this was going to be a new test for my Spanish.

I fumbled with the words for a moment and then said, "Ponga plantanos in el motor." The word for "points" is *platinos*. I had told the man to "put bananas in the motor." Finally, using gestures and pointing I made myself understood, but the mechanic was clearly amused when I left.

Another time, while eating at a restaurant with some Mexican colleagues, I referred to the waitress as *"mono,"* which means monkey, rather than *"mona,"* which means cute. Everyone around me had a good laugh.

When I was ready to begin my field work, Arturo assigned one of his graduate students to help. Over the next few weeks, we visited several cloud forests in Veracruz, but the work was not productive. Sometimes an area of forest I studied one week was gone the next. Giant two-hundred-year-old oaks were cut and burned to make room for planting corn, which, at best in this environment, produced only a few bushels per acre. After a couple of years, the soil became so impoverished it was no longer suitable for growing, so more forest was cut and burned. This cycle had already been repeating for long years before I arrived to study the remnants of the cloud forests.

The first thing I noticed was that desert plants like agave and cacti accustomed to living in dry areas had invaded the regions where cloud forest had been cleared. It occurred to me that perhaps the moisture that had supported the former vegetation was not in the ground but came from thick fog that was swept upward along the mountain slopes and captured by the leaves of the trees. Pines still grew on the uppermost slopes adjacent to an arid plateau above, and I observed that their needles were ideal for combing tiny droplets out of the fog.

Back in Vermont, some of my graduate students were engaged in fog interception research on Camels Hump, and I had been working with them before leaving for Mexico. I decided to conduct an experiment based on what my students and I were learning on Camels Hump to test my hypothesis about the fog-capturing role of cloud forest trees.

Prevailing winds in southeastern Mexico blow westward from the Gulf of Mexico and are forced upward along east-facing slopes of the Sierra Madre Mountains. Most of the moisture in this air falls as rain on the lower slopes where rich farms and forests flourish. As the air rises toward the upper elevations, the rain is depleted, leaving only dense fog. When the fog pushes onto the dry plateaus above, it quickly evaporates if there are no trees to intercept it.

After a year studying and observing the Mexican cloud forests, I returned to Vermont and applied to the Conservation and Research Foundation for a modest grant to further test my fog collecting hypothesis. I was delighted when the foundation awarded me $2,700, which was two hundred dollars more than the request. I immediately contacted my colleagues at the University of Mexico and arranged to do a one-year study using the same procedures my students and I were using to measure fog precipitation in the high elevation forests of Camels Hump. I would make frequent tips to and from Mexico to collect the fog data from the workers there.

Our equipment was simple and inexpensive. It consisted of one-quart oil cans with the tops cut out. One can was fitted with a cylindrical aluminum screen that extended ten inches above the top of the can to simulate the evergreen needles that capture fog droplets. Another can was left open, with no screen. Sets of cans in pairs were placed on posts around the forest. The can without the screen collected rainwater, while the can with the screen collected fog water as well as rainwater. Subtracting the amount of rainwater collected from the total of fog and rainwater together gave a measure of how much water had been combed from the fog alone.

For the Mexican study, I located twelve sites on the slopes of the Sierra Madre Mountains to collect fog. The sites started in Veracruz along the coast and extended to the region above Jalapa in the upper elevations. I also had to locate weather observers who would measure and record the water levels in my collecting equipment on a given day each week for one year. My friends at the University of Mexico helped me find the people and Arturo made up impressive certificates to be given to our workers. He included gold seals and ribbons to indicate the importance of this work.

When I arrived in Mexico to set up the collecting gear, I immediately ran into difficulties. The Mexicans were inexperienced and disorganized, and even simple tasks were challenging and sometimes made more complicated than they needed to be. I was faced with a cultural divide. I wrote a letter to Marie to share my frustrations:

Hotel Stella Maris, Mexico
January 5, 1969

Dear Marie,

Leave at noon for Jalapa and just now I have a few moments to write. Hope you don't mind the diary-like account, like Dad's, but it is the easiest way for me to report. Yesterday was full as I expected and I began to run into the first problem—minor but annoying. It all had to do with the Mexican mind and if you understand it, which I doubt I ever will, it's easier to bear.

When I arrived at the garden in the a.m. to begin assembling equipment, I found plenty of help waiting. I gave instructions about the wooden posts and platforms we need to put the fog devices on. My God, you should see what they came up with! I will need a truck to transport them. The planks would make good coffee tables. Well, I guess they will have to do. Then I needed 30 liter-size oil cans with the ends cut out—a can opener was the obvious answer, but not here. I found four men working on a grinding stone, complete with face masks, grinding out the ends! It took them two hours! Then the oil had to be washed out—they found six space heaters, trucked them into the garden, emptied out the kerosene, and washed them. All of which took precious time. By then it was 2 p.m. and I was getting anxious because the cans had to be painted and calibrated.

Suddenly everyone disappeared except one kid in a dirty red jacket holding a radio to his ear. Where did they go? Home—only work $1/3$ day and not available Sunday and then of course Monday is a holiday which I never heard of. So I was alone—began painting and then came the rain. Paint would not dry so I trucked everything to hotel room, worked until 11 p.m. to finish. Nothing is simple here, as you know.

Feel rested this a.m. and just had breakfast overlooking the art park in front of the hotel. A dozen artists are setting up paintings to exhibit and kids and dogs are running about. So also are some corps of youths who keep jogging past in bunches of eight or so. Plenty of traffic noise and exhaust fumes. Sky overcast and everything wet and chilly from night's rain. Haven't had much chance to look this hotel over but it doesn't seem bad even though it is almost on the corner (two or three blocks away) of Paseo de la Reforma and Ave. Insurgentes.

Looked over the "roof garden and pool," which are misnomers. The garden turns out to be three potted bonsai and the pool half the size of ours in Cuernavaca and two feet deep. But the place is clean beyond belief and is run by a young militant Dutch manager who makes the most of his help. Someone forgot to put soap in my bathroom and I never saw anyone so upset over a bar of soap. Now I find my room is cleaned and tidied two or three times each day. I can tell 'cause the wrinkles on the bed are smoothed after every time I leave the room. I must say that this organization is refreshing in this disorganized society. Chap speaks fluently in six languages and I'm sure this hotel will be one of the best in the city. It is less than a year old and the bar still had to be finished. Just as well because so far I haven't had a chance to use it anyway.

Hope all is well and make sure the kids behave. So far I have not had the chance to do any shopping, which will have to wait until I return from field work. It's impossible to say how long it will take—I have to play it by ear and you know the people.

Love,

Hub

Getting twelve Mexicans to follow the same protocol for one year was a challenge, but they were remarkably conscientious, and they contributed to gathering the data I needed to prove my theory.

On the lower mountain slopes, the cans with and without screens collected equal amounts of water, but on the upper slopes, the cans with screens collected much more than the cans without screens. This extra water came from fog. So I was right: it was the fog moisture collected by trees in the cloud forest that made the difference here between forest and desert. Over the centuries, the removal of trees in the cloud forest had created thousands of acres of high-altitude desert. My experiment was successful and it was one of the best experiences of my career. More recently, such research has been expanded in fog-prone areas of the world and, looking back, I feel fortunate to have been one of the early pioneers.

The house on Tuscarora Road. Special Collections, UVM Bailey-Howe Library.

A victory ship, Winthrop Victory, similar to the Pass Christian Victory that carried heifers to Poland

Photo of Hub at age sixteen, the year he traveled with the heifers to Poland. Special Collections, UVM Bailey-Howe Library.

South Buffalo High School

Marie and Hub at the North Java Farm. Special Collections, UVM Bailey-Howe Library.

Pierre Dansereau,
Michigan.
Special Collections,
UVM Bailey-Howe
Library.

Primrose, Michigan.
Special Collections, UVM
Bailey-Howe Library.

Hub at Knob Lake (1957).
Special Collections, UVM
Bailey-Howe Library.

Marie at Knob Lake (1957).
Special Collections, UVM Bailey-
Howe Library.

A campsite in Hoosier Pass, Colorado (1954), with the car Hub and Marie bought from Hub's dad. Special Collections, UVM Bailey-Howe Library.

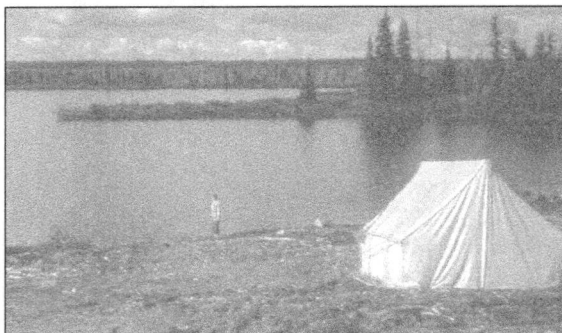

A campsite on Knob Lake (1957). Special Collections, UVM Bailey-Howe Library.

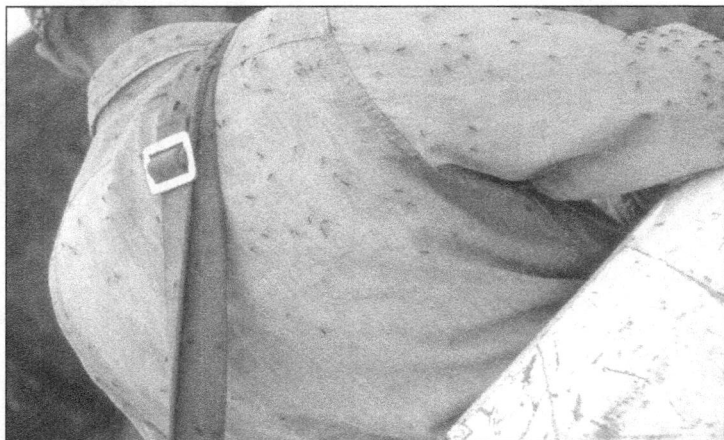

Mosquitoes at Knob Lake (1957). Special Collections, UVM Bailey-Howe Library.

Switch-backs on mountain roads, Colombia (1965).
Special Collections, UVM Bailey-Howe Library.

George Feuerbringer's home in the mountains of
Colombia (1965). Special Collections, UVM Bailey-Howe
Library.

Doel Suharto demonstrates drinking water from a vine in Colombian forest (1965). Special Collections, UVM Bailey-Howe Library.

George Feuerbringer's monkey, Ramon, Colombia

George Fuerbringer's parrot, Colombia

Special Collections, UVM Bailey-Howe Library.

Demonstrating ocean fishing, Hub lands two striped bass at Bailey Island, Maine (1978). Photo by John Olsen.

Hub and Marie (c. 1970s)

II.
Life on
Schillhammer Road

We Buy an Old Farm

All my life, thoughts of living in the country have tugged at my heart. My father's farm instilled in me an even deeper desire to own a piece of earth, though I still question whether a person can own nature. But for as long as I can remember, "country" has meant meadows, pastures, and forests with all the wonderful plant and animal life growing there.

Settling in Vermont, I began to feel that my dream might really come true, a dream that Marie now shared. When I wasn't busy teaching botany at the University of Vermont, we searched for just the right quiet place in the country where I could plant a half-acre garden and keep my bees.

It took over two years of looking, with increasingly frustrated realtors, but we finally found a match for our dream. A realtor who knew the farming community well took us to the little town of Jericho, where a dairy farmer on Schillhammer Road was about to go out of business.

We went to see the farm in winter, approaching the farm in a blinding snowstorm, making our way down a winding dirt road on the outskirts of Jericho village. The realtor parked the car out of sight of the farmhouse and said, "Stay here. Let me visit my friend first." He knew best.

We waited in the cold for twenty minutes or so until the he returned to announce, "He'll sell!"

I was ecstatic, even though I couldn't see anything except the thick snow falling all around us. Somehow I knew that this was where I wanted to be. We wrapped our coats around us and walked up the tree-lined road to see the place and meet the owner. After brief negotiations, Marie and I bought the farm—90 acres "more or less," two barns, and a weathered farmhouse without a working flush toilet.

We moved into the farmhouse that February, one of the coldest months of the year in Vermont. A huge wood furnace in the basement devoured cords of wood but delivered little heat. The house was a wreck: ceilings were collapsing, floors were warped, and the interior was dark and dismal, especially the kitchen, which had a black cast iron sink dominating one end.

But we weren't discouraged. The first thing I did was build a sandbox in the living room to entertain our two small boys while Marie and I thought about what we'd do to make the house livable. The important thing to both of us was that we now had our own farm. We knew we could restore the house in time.

I still recall the first sunny day that spring. I was lying beside Marie in the hayfield gazing up at the blue sky and feeling that life couldn't get any better than it was right then.

We now owned land on both sides of Schillhammer Road, with our barn on one side and the house on the other, well out of sight of any neighbors. We enjoyed the quiet and privacy, but I worried that someday the Schillhammer Farm—our closest neighbor—would be sold to a developer and we'd lose the solitude we so enjoyed. To forestall the intrusions of this anticipated event, I planted 10,000 pines and spruces between our land and our neighbor's. Today these trees are forty feet tall, creating a formidable hedge along that original boundary.

Across the road from our house, there's a wooded rise called Laisdell Hill. Our farm ended at the base of the hill, and I got to worrying that someday the hilltop might sprout a tower or even a vacation home. Either would spoil our view and diminish our special part of Jericho, so when the land was offered for sale, we bought another twenty-five acres "more or less" (this is the way farmlands are typically described on deeds in Vermont), including all of the hillside we could see from our farm.

Years later, my elderly neighbor, Martha Fuller, who owned the Schillhammer Farm, decided to sell and we bought her property, too, which added another two hundred acres—more or less.

According to town records, we now owned 323 acres, eight of them thanks to "more" rather than "less" in our various parcels. Because the Schillhammer Farm also included land on both sides of the road, we now had all the protection we would ever need to preserve one of the most picturesque back roads in one of the fastest growing areas in Vermont.

Over the years, I used our farm as a field laboratory for my ecology classes and my students spent many hours studying plant succession in our abandoned cow pasture that, left to its own devices, was slowly returning to the forest. In one experiment, we placed quadrats over old cow pies and counted the different plants inside the spaces to see if there were more species growing near a cow pie than in non-pie sites. Yes, there were—the cow pies always won.

Other times we inventoried wildflowers in the woods, and at the end of a hot day we'd retire to the farmhouse where Marie served cold lemonade to grateful students. My own taxonomic skills were always at work as I inventoried all the plant species in the hayfields and forest. It was satisfying to know that everything I identified belonged to me— and that my dream of becoming a part-time farmer had come true.

One year, our oldest son Tom's girlfriend gave him a calf, and I began an unexpected phase of this career—as a part-time rancher. We raised Tom's calf, finally selling it to a cattle dealer, but in the meantime, I had become fascinated by the idea of developing a cattle ranch right here in Vermont. I began to buy Black Angus cows with the intention of breeding them and selling the calves.

My cows dutifully produced calves each spring, which I sold on schedule at the end of the summer, but I found it difficult to do year-round chores on the ranch while carrying a full time teaching load at the University. So our sons pitched in. By now we had three—our youngest, Andy, having been born four years after we bought our farm.

Together we would mow the hayfields and rake, bale, and haul load after load to the barn. It was hot, sweaty, dusty work, but my young sons worked hard and did their best, which made me proud of them. We added two pigs to the livestock we raised each year, and together with a cow we slaughtered for our own freezer, plus what we grew in the garden, our hardworking sons were always well fed.

The cattle operation lasted seventeen years—too long, with me losing money on it nearly every year. But I learned a lot about the ordeals of farmers and ranchers who are at the mercy of weather, cattle diseases, and economic forces over which they have no control. I made money in only two of those seventeen years, when I sold sides of beef myself rather than sending my live cows to the cattle auction.

This education as a farmer and rancher added to my professional education as a botanist, and I look back on those early years with satisfaction and pleasure. Life here has been rich and rewarding almost without exception.

The one painful memory attached to the farm is the devastating moment in 1999, when Marie died suddenly and unexpectedly, just a day before our 48th wedding anniversary.

I miss her greatly to this day and only wish she could have seen the successful lives of our three sons. All three have become scientists— Tom and Jim are botanists and Andy's an atmospheric physicist. Tom and Jim also married botanists, and Tom is now Dean of the College of Agriculture and Life Sciences at UVM, after serving as chairman of the Botany Department, the position I held for twenty years.

Marie is the one who made it all possible, taking on the care of our growing family while I, as a young scientist, explored the botanical world from North America to the Canadian Arctic, to the upper Amazon and Andes Mountains of South America, and finally to the cloud forests of Mexico.

Marie always supported my work. When we were young, she often traveled with me to remote areas where we camped under spare and difficult conditions. She never complained, even when eventually I'd be gone on my own for weeks at a time, leaving her home to care for our three boys.

During a discussion of our lives and careers, my brother-in-law once asked me what I would do if I could live my life all over again. That was easy. "I would marry Marie, raise three boys, teach botany, and tend my garden and bees on Schillhammer Road."

I couldn't have had it any better.

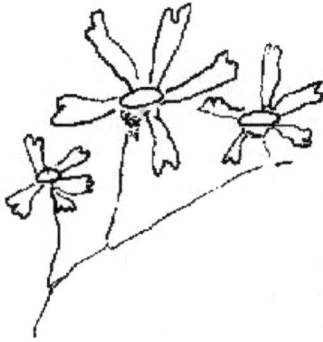

Our Well

L ike most of the farms and residences along Schillhammer Road, we get our water from a shallow well. Ours is fourteen feet deep, and the well at the old Schillhammer Farm next door is only sixteen feet. But the water reaching taps at both places is delicious—clear, sparkling, and cold. I measured its temperature and I discovered that it's 43 degrees—same as the average annual temperature here and cold enough to condense droplets on the outside of a glass.

I've since learned these shallow country wells spring up in deep glacial till that was deposited about 12,000 years ago, and as far as I can tell they produce an endless supply of fresh water. The Schillhammer Farm's well once supplied enough water for twenty five dairy cows plus all the other needs of the farm and household, and it never went dry. I also learned that shallow wells in this part of Vermont often have better water quality than drilled wells of a hundred feet or more. The water at greater depths sometimes contains more iron or sulfur that alters the taste and stains laundry.

The water table in our area—the upper level of the groundwater that my well depends on—fluctuates during the year. It's highest in spring when snowmelt and spring rains saturate the soil, and lowest in the drier seasons of late summer and fall. I visualize an underground lake that rises and falls in this annual cycle.

When we first bought our farm back in the 1950s, I worried about the supply of water needed to wash clothes and dishes, take showers, flush toilets, and meet whatever other demands my growing family would place on our shallow well. To find out what the water table was doing, I regularly took the wooden cover off the well and dropped a weighted string to the bottom. Retrieving the string, I measured the wet portion to get the water depth. In March it would be almost fourteen feet deep, and in September and November recede to about three feet. During one exceptionally dry season, it went to a mere one foot. Watching and measuring, I learned that starting from a full well in spring, the water table dropped about an inch a day regardless of how much water we used. It reached a low point and then would begin to recover in the fall. Water drawn during the day could lower the level one or two inches for that day, but the well always recharged overnight.

During severe droughts or shortages, we tried to limit how much we drew from the well at one time, but I realized we couldn't save water from day to day by rationing. However much we used, it would continue to come back to its own level—a great relief to me, raising a family of three boys, all of them taking showers, flushing toilets, and needing their clothing washed.

The structure of our well itself is a work of stone art. The bottom is six feet across and tapers upward to about three feet at the top. The stones are carefully placed to form a stable cone. Assuming that our well was built at about the same time as our house, it's now almost two hundred years old, yet all the original stones are still in place—a remarkable feat of engineering. There is another shallow well near an apple tree at the edge of our hayfield. It's constructed just like the one we still use, but the one in the field had long ago been filled with rocks to prevent people or animals from falling in.

I sometimes wonder about the stone craftsmen who built these wells. They must have been in great demand during the early years of settlement when there were no such things as drilled wells. How they decided where to locate these old wells is a mystery to me. Did the farmers use a forked willow branch as a divining rod, or simply look for indicator plants such as willows and rushes to decide where to dig? Or maybe it was just good luck, since clay-laden glacial till holds lots of water anyway, so wherever you dig, there's a chance you can find water to fill the bottom of the hole. However they chose the spot, our well located between two big hundred-year-old sugar maples has always produced all the water we need.

During one unusually dry summer, I observed that in mid-September the water table began to rise even though there was no rain. At the same time, I noticed the leaves on nearby maples and other trees were showing color and beginning to fall. Was there a connection?

I speculated that the corky abscission layer that forms at the base of leaf stalks at this time of year and lessens the amount of moisture flowing into the leaves had reduced the amount of water the trees drew from the soil. That might have accounted for the unexpected rise in the water table.

During another unusually dry summer, I needed to replace a float valve on the intake pipe at the bottom of our well. The water level was only two feet, so I lowered a ladder and climbed down to the bottom. I could stand there and see the tapering stone sides all around me and blue sky through the opening above. Beneath my feet, I could see emerald green water bubbling through sand and gravel. It was a wonderful moment that has stayed with me and when I draw a glass of water from my kitchen tap, I often recall where it came from. That makes it taste even better.

Our Pond

We dreamed of having a trout pond somewhere on our property and soon after we bought it we found a corner of wet pasture across the road from the house that seemed suitable for pond construction. But an extension specialist from the University tested the soil and said it wouldn't hold water.

Unfazed, I noted that wet-loving plants such as pussy willows and alders were growing in that corner, which meant there was plenty of water there. So I decided I'd just trust the soil. Dismissing the advice of the pond expert, we hired a bulldozer and went to work.

In a few days, the dozer had cleared brush and grass from an acre, and as it dug deeper water began to flow into the excavation. In one spot, it actually gushed into the hole like a broken fire hydrant.

Our new pond filled within weeks and we stocked it with brook trout for that season. The next year, I wanted to stock it again, but I worried that the older trout would cannibalize the new ones. I asked the operator at the fish hatchery what size fish an older trout would eat. He was a wonderful old Vermonter with a withered face. He opened his toothless mouth as wide as possible and pointed his finger inside, indicating clearly that a trout would eat anything it could get into its mouth. We bought the fish anyway.

Later that week, I was visiting our trout pond when I heard a thrashing of water near the bank. I saw that a ten-inch trout had grabbed an eighteen-inch garter snake by its head. The snake coiled around the trout, and again and again the trout dove to the bottom of the pond. Finally they disappeared for good and I thought I had lost a trout. But two days later, I was standing on the shore and I saw a trout swim slowly by with a long white streamer extending from its anus. It was the skin of the snake that had passed through the trout's entire alimentary canal.

I told my boys about it. "Next time you go swimming, you'd better watch out!" I said. Today our pond is full of trout, and despite that snake-eater it has always provided a safe and refreshing place to swim, first for our boys and now for our grandchildren.

Years after we dug the first pond, we decided to add another one. There's a beautiful twenty-acre field behind the house that has been a productive hayfield since farmers first started farming here. When we bought the property in 1958, the county agent told me it was one of the best hayfields in the area, but I noticed a wet area in one corner. Every summer when my boys and I hayed, either the tractor or the hay wagon got stuck in that wet spot. Finally a neighboring farmer suggested I put a duck pond there, and that's exactly what I did. Once again, I hired a bulldozer to scrape a hole—only half an acre this time—and once again the hole soon filled with water.

Our duck pond was ready, but the ducks didn't come to it immediately. The first winter, the surface froze over smooth and good for skating. Family and friends played ice hockey until the heavy snows came that were difficult to clear. After the ice melted in the spring, I thought the pond looked inviting enough to attract a stray duck or two to nest there. Occasionally a pair of mallards did show up, but they cruised around the edges and then flew away. Once in a while mergansers stopped by. They were fun to watch as they dove deep into the water, surfaced, and dove again. I hoped they might nest, but they never did.

Although no ducks had chosen our pond for nesting, it became a mecca for other wildlife. Moose left their tracks along the soft, grassy edges. Sometimes wild turkeys stood on the rim preening their feathers. I've watched the males trying to get the attention of the females by fanning their colorful tails. The hens paid no attention and just kept feeding on the grasses and sedges along the margins of the pond.

Spring peepers, wood frogs, and toads invaded our pond. At night, their mating calls were almost deafening. One day I saw hundreds of mating wood frogs form a swirling mass at the edge of the pond. The orgy lasted two days and then they were gone, leaving their gelatinous egg masses behind. How hundreds of frogs can disappear so completely when they've finished mating, I have no idea and I haven't checked into it, but I'm pleased to think they must be living their invisible lives somewhere on my land.

Once a pair of Canada geese visited the pond. I took corn over and scattered it in the shallow water near the edges for them. The geese feasted on underwater kernels that the crows couldn't reach. The arrival of the geese each morning was heralded by frantic honking. Then, like two jet fighters, they'd zoom in over the rim of the pond and hit the water with a great splash. After feeding, they'd stand on the pond's edge, preening their feathers and taking a long rest. Late in the afternoon, they'd start honking again and prepare to take off, with yet more honking. They'd soar in a wide circle over the hayfield, turn west, and head to the Winooski River to spend the night. Once they departed, I quickly took another can of corn to the pond and scattered it in the water for the next day's visit.

At dawn I could hear them coming again, honking and honking some more as they approached. It was a wonderful sound to my ears. Later in the day, I would catch sight of them as they stood on the rim of our pond. I always found them beautiful, with their long black necks held erect to show off white chin straps.

Thinking that ducks might prefer their nests to be surrounded by water to deter predators, my boys and I constructed a small floating island made from a wooden pallet with Styrofoam panels. We floated it out to the center of the pond, anchored it with cinder blocks, and covered our island with hay and hemlock branches that we thought would look inviting. Still no ducks came.

Weeks later, our first ducks finally arrived—from a distance and on foot! But even they were only visiting, not nesting there.

My son Tom now lives in the old Schillhammer house about a quarter mile up the road from my farm. A large red maple stands at the edge of his driveway, and I had noticed a deep cavity in the trunk about halfway up, at the point where several large branches spread over the road. On one of my morning walks, I saw a wood duck pass right over my head and plunge into the cavity where it must have had a nest. Later that day, Tom reported seeing a small duckling under a rhubarb leaf in his garden, about fifty feet from the tree. The next morning I visited the pond to see a female wood duck with ten little ducklings perched on our wooden island. She herded them into the water and they swam to the far shore. What amazes me is that these ducklings had managed to travel a quarter of a mile overland, passing through a dense, grassy hayfield, climbing over a vine-covered stone wall, crossing a shrubby fencerow, and then traveling the width of another hayfield to reach our pond. (Actually, as remarkable as that quarter-mile trek was for these ducklings, it doesn't compare with the distance goslings travel, as reported by Bernd Heinrich in his book *The Geese on Beaver Bog*. He observed goslings traveling two and a half miles to reach a new home.)

I still wish a duck family would nest on our pond, but so far we've had just visitors. While I'm waiting, I'll continue to spread corn. Someday our pond may yet become the true duck pond I intended it to be.

My Garden: Potatoes

My first vegetable garden on Schillhammer Road was a great success. The soil was more fertile than I expected, and I grew broccoli heads as big as cabbages. As a botanist, I wanted to try growing all kinds of vegetables, including those not commonly found in supermarkets— things like celeriac, kohlrabi, and kale. I also experimented with different fertilizers, one year growing squashes in hills fertilized with cow manure, horse manure, or barn swallow guano collected from piles in our barn. The results: the cow manure won, while the swallow guano failed completely because some animal dug it up and ate it.

Over many years experimenting with vegetables, fertilizers, and anything else that occurred to me, I learned three things about myself as a gardener: the potato is absolutely my favorite vegetable; I can't for the life of me grow a radish; and I have a complicated relationship with woodchucks.

First, my beloved potatoes. Each year I grow about twenty varieties and, over the years, I have grown about seventy different types altogether. I've grown Kennebeck, Burbank Russet, Yukon Gold, Red Norland, Russian Banana, Purple Marker, All Red, All Blue, Cranberry Red, Fingerlings, German Butterball, Rose Finn Apple, and lots more. My favorite early potato, which I dig up early in July, is Red Norland, with its small succulent tubers and sweet earthy taste. A second planting of Red Norland can be started in mid-July or early August, which gives enough growing time to produce a delicious crop in mid-September. Later in the season, it's the firm and starchy Kennebeck.

Most varieties taste much the same but there are some differences in color, texture, and shape. Russets have thick skins, are mealy, and

91

make good bakers, while Kennebecks make the best mashed potatoes to my taste. Yukon Golds have yellow flesh making them look as if they've already been buttered, and both Yukon Golds and Kennebecks are good winter keepers. The shapes of most potatoes are round to oblong, but Russian Banana and other fingerlings are slender and elongated. Rose Finn Apple produces the strangest forms of all, sometimes sprouting branches of small elongated tubers that extend from the main tuber like arms and legs. They look like "potato men."

I love to dig my potatoes. When I turn the soil, out pop the plump tubers as if by magic. I find it hard to imagine how, in just a few months, the earth can produce such a splendid product. While digging, I anticipate the many delicious ways we will enjoy the harvest—baked, boiled, mashed, roasted, scalloped, French fried, and cut up into a salad. My potato crop is always colorful. I grow red, white, blue, and purple varieties, which make a great display even before I cook them.

Just as squirrels store nuts to provide food for the winter, I store potatoes. Our cool, moist cellar is lined with bushels of them, each basket neatly labeled. In the middle of winter, it gives me great pleasure to visit the cellar and gaze at my hoard.

Most North Americans are familiar with only the Idaho or Maine potatoes sold at grocery stores, but there are over three hundred species and 4,500 potato varieties worldwide. A seed bank in Lima, Peru, keeps eighty percent of the known varieties in hermetically sealed tubes at 6° C to perpetuate the genetic varieties and guarantee their preservation.

Potatoes have a long and, to me, fascinating history, originating in the Andes Mountains of South America, where they were cultivated 2,000 years ago by the Inca Indians. Potatoes prefer cool, moist conditions and, in the Andes, they grow at elevations up to 12,000 feet. They were a prized food for the Incas, who freeze-dried them in the frosty higher elevations to make *chuño*, a light, starchy food that was easily carried and stored.

Spaniards searching for gold discovered potatoes and sent them back to Europe where, by 1588, they had spread from Spain to France, Germany, and Ireland. At first potatoes weren't accepted as food because they belonged to the Solanaceae, the nightshade family, and were thought to be poisonous. Even the renowned naturalist, Linnaeus, said "Beware the Solanaceae." In Scotland potatoes were scorned because they weren't mentioned in the Bible, but eventually they became accepted as a staple throughout Europe because they were easy to grow, nutritious, and would keep over the winter. Poor people became dependent on them as their main food source, and when the potato blight—a fungus infection of the plants and tubers—struck Europe in 1847 wiping out potato crops, an estimated three million people starved. Indeed, it was during this period that many thousands of people from Europe, especially from Ireland and Germany, migrated to the United States.

Some years ago, I acquired a potato from the Yucatan with a smooth skin and slightly yellow flesh. I was able to plant some of this variety in my garden, but the potatoes they produced were disappointingly small—about the size of a marble. The following year I planted the "marbles," hoping they'd grow larger; they did, but only slightly. For seven years I planted my Yucatan crop, and each year the tubers were larger than the last, until finally they reached the size of the originals, about as big as golf balls. I speculate that the length of the day is a factor in potato development and, in Vermont, summer days are much longer than they are in the tropics. Over time, my Yucatan potatoes became physiologically adapted to our increased sunlight. That they were good eating was confirmed the year squirrels invaded my cellar and chose to devour them in preference to all my other varieties.

Botanically, the potato is a tuber, or fleshy, modified stem and not actually a root. The "eye" of a potato is a vegetative bud that, when planted, will grow into a succulent, bushy plant. Late in the season, potato flowers produce small, round, fruits that look like green cherry tomatoes. Each fruit contains hundreds of seeds, but when planted, they don't yield the same variety of potato that produced the seed. During pollination, potato genes in the flowers become so mixed that each seed carries a different genetic make-up and won't produce the same variety from which it came. To maintain a variety, potatoes must be grown vegetatively from the pieces with eyes that don't cross pollinate.

Here in Vermont, my potato's main enemy is the Colorado potato beetle. This miserable pest supposedly followed wagon tracks left by early settlers. While the settlers were headed west, the beetles headed east, migrating from their natural western habitat to become pests in eastern gardens. The adult beetles don't eat the leaves of potato plants, but the newly hatched larvae do. After mating, adult females lay clusters of yellow eggs on the tender leaves, and when the eggs hatch in a few days, the hungry orange grubs chomp away until the leaves are reduced to skeletons.

Potato beetles have become resistant to most pesticides and are difficult to control. I try to keep them in check by walking down the rows and picking adult beetles from the plants, hoping to catch them before they mate or lay their eggs. Another technique involves timing. The adult beetles overwinter in the ground and emerge in late spring, just when an early planting of potatoes offers them leaves at their juicy best. The population of beetles builds from mid-June to the first week in July, at which time it crashes. During their peak, I've collected as many as 120 beetles a day. After the first week of July, however, the numbers drop to twenty or fewer, so my second technique for controlling potato beetles is to plant after the first week in July. I avoid the population surge while still allowing enough time for a good harvest. Also, since potato beetles overwinter in the soil, I've learned to rotate my crop and plant potatoes in new areas where I haven't grown them before.

Something else I've noticed—adult beetles seem to prefer to lay their eggs on red potato varieties. These varieties might serve to collect and trap large numbers of beetles and might even offer a way to develop a new control. If a researcher were to determine the substance in red potato plants that attracts the beetles, a creative company could produce a synthetic version to lure beetles away from the potato patch. Also noted: as the season progresses, the color of the beetles becomes darker, especially at the end of June. I wonder if a different variety matures in late June, or if the change in temperature or the length of the day causes this change in color. Anyway, it's an observable phenomenon, and some summer I'll collect the beetles over the season to document my observation.

Beetles or not, I love my potatoes and will continue to grow and enjoy them as long as I'm alive. Radishes, however, are a different story.

My Garden: Radishes

I cannot grow a radish. Much as I love gardening, and as willing as I am to experiment with all kinds of vegetables, varieties, and techniques, the radish does not grow. As if to tease me, a recent Gurney's Seed Catalog said, "Fast growing radishes often are the first ready-to-harvest crop of the season. So easy even children can plant and care for them."

So why is it that I, a retired professor with a Ph.D. in botany, cannot grow a radish? I'm thinking maybe it's to keep me humble.

My earliest experience with radishes was back in childhood. My first grade teacher, who wanted our class to appreciate growing plants, gave us all some radish seeds. I took them home, planted them, and was impressed that my seeds germinated in only a couple of days. They grew quite nicely in their pot until they were about an inch tall, and then Bingo, the family cat, ate them.

But I learned that radishes do indeed grow fast and, if Bingo hadn't eaten those first plants, I might have been able to harvest them in only three weeks. But something is wrong between me and radishes—even as a child I consistently failed to produce the plump red ones my first grade classmates managed to grow.

My current garden in Jericho is about a quarter of an acre in size and crammed with about as many kinds of vegetables as you can name—celery, carrots, lettuce, five kinds of tomatoes, six kinds of peppers, twenty varieties of potatoes, and lots more—but nary a radish.

My first attempt to grow radishes here on Schillhammer road yielded nothing more than leaves and flowers. The plants produced no fleshy roots at all. Then I learned that radishes are long-day plants, which means that when days lengthen, radishes put all their energy into their flowers rather than into plump, edible roots.

So the next March, when the days were still short, I carefully scraped the lingering snow off a corner of my garden and planted radish seeds. They germinated, made lots of leaves and flowers—but still no radishes. Thinking maybe my problem was in the soil, I neutralized the acidity and worked bushels of sand into the heavy loam to make it lighter and more arable. I planted more radishes and again I got leaves and flowers.

Next came fertilizer trials—and leaves and flowers.

I searched for a foolproof variety that would work even for me, trying French Breakfast, Cherry Belle, Champion, and White Icicle, but none of them produced an edible root, only leaves and flowers.

In the meantime, my neighbor, Martha Fuller, planted and harvested beautiful radishes in her tiny garden every year. Martha was delighted to know I couldn't grow them. When I visited her during the radish season, she would display her crop on the kitchen table with an impish smile. For several years, my middle son, Jim, who holds a Ph.D. in botany from Indiana University and lives in Sioux Falls, South Dakota, would send me a package of big, beautiful radishes grown in his own garden. When he didn't send the actual radishes, he would mail a photograph of himself holding a handful of his monsters.

Martha is gone now and my oldest son, Tom, and his wife live on her farm where they've developed their own sizable garden. Tom, who has a Ph.D. in botany from Syracuse University, now brings *his* radishes over to my house each spring, spreading his bounty out on my kitchen counter. Is it because I got my Ph.D. at the University of Michigan, or am I just jinxed?

I've given up trying to grow radishes and just buy them at the supermarket. Whatever my contributions to this world as a botanist and gardener, growing radishes will not be among them. Every time I buy a package of grocery store radishes, I am humbled by the reminder that there are some things I can't control. Which brings me to the story of a woodchuck named Woody.

My Garden: Woody the Woodchuck

I'd actually rather not tell the story of the woodchuck I named Woody, but the events surrounding him weigh heavily on my mind.

Gardening is my hobby—a passion, if not an obsession. I am highly aware that I'm running out of time and will be fortunate to have another ten gardens before I die. Every spring is therefore precious to me, as is every plant in my garden.

These days I grow about seventy-five different varieties of vegetables. I sow the seeds in flats in my greenhouse in March and nurture them until they can be planted in the outdoor garden in May. Because my garden is big, it requires lots of cultivating and weeding. In the best of years, it's a challenge to grow a garden as big as mine here in northern Vermont where we have to contend with all kinds of threats.

First, there's the unpredictable weather. Some years there's too much rainfall and others, too little, Temperatures fluctuate from too hot to too cold, and an occasional late frost hits my garden in June. Then there's the constant fight against insect pests like Colorado potato beetles and cabbage worms.

Mammals take their toll. Deer relish my kale and brussels sprouts, and one recent summer a moose paid a visit, leaving a trail of massive footprints right across the garden. In fact, it takes constant and considerable effort to bring my vegetables along until they're ready for harvest. And my most dreaded enemy is the woodchuck.

Woodchucks are eating machines. They can devour a bushel of vegetables in a day. One woodchuck cleaned out my entire kohlrabi patch in a single afternoon. I've tried to live-trap them, but I've never been able to lure them into the elaborate box trap that I built. I even baited it with broccoli, carrots, and other favorite vegetables, but the woodchucks pay no attention to a well-stocked trap.

In recent years the garden's been free of woodchucks, perhaps because they're hunted by a pack of coyotes that now live in the woods near my house. But one day I looked out my window and saw a young woodchuck emerge from the tall grass at the edge of the flower garden and head toward my vegetables. By the time I rushed out to chase it away, it had already eaten five full brussels sprout plants.

Of all the plants to choose, the brussels sprout seeds I'd started earlier in the spring hadn't germinated well and it was already too late to start over again, so I was going to need every single plant to make a decent sprout crop. And now five plants were gone.

For the next week, everyone in my family was on the lookout for the woodchuck I had started to call Woody. But Woody was nowhere to be seen and we hoped the coyotes had dined on him.

I wondered what I should do if he returned and thought about the old .22-caliber rifle that I'd bought when I was in high school. My parents didn't like guns but they allowed me to buy this one for target shooting. I added a telescopic sight and enjoyed the precision of shooting at inanimate targets, but by now I hadn't fired the rifle for at least thirty years. Basically I'm a pacifist and don't like to kill things, so the rifle had been hiding in the back corner of my closet gathering dust. Feeling the threat of that woodchuck, however, I retrieved the rifle and propped it next to the back door that leads out to my garden. I truly hoped I wouldn't have to use it, but having it there gave me some comfort.

Every day I asked if anyone had seen Woody. For two weeks, there was no sign of him. Then I noticed that the leaves on my broccoli plants were chewed, and some of the plants were even shredded. Woody had returned.

My tension mounted as I thought about what he might destroy next.

One day in June, I arose at daybreak and looked out the second story window that overlooks my garden. It was one of those beautiful quiet mornings with a clear blue sky and dew glistening on the grass. I looked out over the back lawn that gave way to the garden and was delighted with the view, until I spotted Woody.

He was on the lawn happily eating tender grass shoots and clover blossoms. I watched him for a moment and then he began to lumber toward the garden. In a panic I rushed downstairs, grabbed the rifle and quietly opened the back door. Woody had moved into the tall grass at the edge of the garden. I carefully raised the rifle and lined up the crosshairs. Slowly, oh, so slowly, I squeezed the trigger.

A sharp crack shattered the quiet of dawn. Woody's leg rose in the air, and I knew I had hit him. At that moment a flock of blackbirds passed over and swooped down, fluttering and squawking over the dying woodchuck. They knew something terrible had happened.

Why am I still bothered by it? Woody was a wild native animal who didn't see a difference between the vegetables in my garden and the grass shoots and clover blossoms on the lawn. He seemed so totally happy in his woodchuck world. Who was I to take his life? The question still haunts me.

My son Tom buried Woody in a shallow grave at a corner of the vegetable garden he'd loved, and I tried to forget what I'd done. The next day, Tom happened by Woody's grave and saw that something had dug him up and eaten him. That knowledge actually eased my guilt a bit, but I'm still uncomfortable about shooting him. I'm hoping the coyotes will save me from ever having to do it again.

Bird Feeders

Although I'm a botanist by training, I've always been interested in wildlife, too. My back porch is testimony to how much I enjoy having various kinds of animals—except for woodchucks—hanging around my house. The floor is made of old bricks with weeds flourishing in the cracks, which seem to make animal visitors feel right at home. Then there's a dense thicket of viburnum and mock orange that crowds against the porch edge offering plenty of shade and cover. Beyond that are more shrubs, including lilacs and beauty bushes, that offer yet more protective cover. My landscaping may look messy to human eyes, but it's highly attractive to wildlife, especially since I offer an ample supply of sunflower seeds year round.

Two tube feeders hang from the porch ceiling, both of which I fill daily with premium black oil sunflower seeds. Each feeder has six holes and six perches where birds can land to feed or extract seeds and take them somewhere else to eat them. I marvel at how small birds like goldfinches are able to crack open the hard shells of sunflower seeds despite their small beaks. I've observed how they use their beaks strategically to turn the seed to just the right position to crack the shell and reach the kernel inside. Other birds with bigger beaks crack seeds faster and more efficiently than goldfinches, but they make a bigger mess. I've watched evening and rose-breasted grosbeaks open as many as ten or more sunflower seeds a minute, sending the empty shells flying in all directions.

Over the years I've noticed that each species of bird has its own distinctive behavior at the feeder. Nuthatches select a single seed and fly to a nearby tree, where they push the seed into a crack in the bark and peck away at the shell. My favorite, a downy woodpecker, stuffs a seed into a nail hole on one of the wooden porch posts and pecks away at it right there where I can watch the whole process through my kitchen window. Blue jays are too big to stand comfortably on the feeder perches, but they can cling to one just long enough to stuff several seeds into their crops before flying to a tree branch. There they disgorge the seeds one at a time, clasping each in turn against the branch with their claws while they open it.

Some birds feed mostly on the porch floor and depend on fallen seeds for their food. Red-winged blackbirds strut around on the bricks, their red and yellow epaulets showing brightly as they sound their raspy calls and hunt for sunflower chips that have been left behind. Song sparrows, chipping sparrows, and mourning doves compete with the redwings for the seeds that litter my porch floor. The only problem bird is a hairy woodpecker that balances on a perch and hammers away at the feeder just as it would hammer on a tree to find insects. Seeds fly in all directions, fast diminishing the supply inside the feeder but delighting the birds, squirrels, and chipmunks waiting below.

Speaking of squirrels, they're worse than the hairy woodpecker. They shinny up a post and leap onto one of the feeders, sending down an even bigger shower of seeds. Down below, they compete with the birds, chipmunks, and other squirrels for the seeds they've scattered. I've seen as many as seven red squirrels and five chipmunks scrambling around my porch floor at the same time. I like to watch what they do with the seeds they claim. The squirrels stay right where they are, sitting on their haunches and deftly holding each seed in their front paws while they eat it. Chipmunks, on the other hand, scurry about stuffing seeds into their cheek pouches until they can get no more in. Then, with cheeks bulging, they rush off the porch and disappear briefly to cache their store for eating later.

Watching the chipmunks that visit my porch reminds me of a boyhood prank. When I was growing up in Buffalo, our family had our milk delivered in glass bottles that narrowed near the top. My brother and I would put peanuts into an empty bottle to attract chipmunks into it. Then we'd watch them stuff their cheek pouches so full they were too big to get out. It was a nasty trick, but chipmunks aren't stupid. They'd eat the peanuts and escape unharmed.

Recently I learned something new about chipmunks. I noticed dense clumps of sunflower seedlings growing in my asparagus patch and wondered what they were doing there. Then I remembered the chipmunks who had disappeared from the porch with bulging cheeks. I figured these clumps of sunflower seedlings must have been planted by chipmunks. I dug up some clumps to see how many seeds were in each one to get an idea of how many seeds a chipmunk can stuff into its cheek pouches. The totals ranged from 26 to 105!

Because 105 seemed like a lot of seeds for one chipmunk's cheeks, I decided to run a test. I counted out 200 black oil sunflower seeds and placed them in a pile on the porch where I could watch what happened. Soon a chipmunk approached the pile and began stuffing its face. I watched its cheeks grow bigger and bigger and finally, when it couldn't get any more in, it scurried away to the asparagus patch. I counted the remaining seeds and discovered there were 95, which means a chipmunk's cheek pouches can definitely hold 105 seeds. Five minutes later the chipmunk was back for the rest of the pile.

I looked up chipmunks' food habits and I learned that eastern chipmunks typically store food in their underground burrows, but some young chipmunks and females rearing young engage in what's called *scatter hoarding*. They bury loads of seeds in shallow holes around their territories and camouflage them with soil and litter. If the seeds stored in their burrows are stolen by other chipmunks, these scatter hoards provide a back-up supply. If a scatter hoard isn't retrieved, it can sprout—as several did in my asparagus patch.

I enjoy my messy porch and the activity it invites, even the hairy woodpecker I have to chase from the feeders to keep him from emptying them. After all these years, I've discovered there are still new things for me to learn—like exactly how many black oil sunflower seeds a chipmunk can stuff into its cheek pouches at one time.

Bees

I've been a beekeeper since I was twelve years old and the complex life of a bee colony has never ceased to amaze me.

There are about 60,000 honey bees in a typical colony, and their organization is a model of efficiency. Thousands of worker bees care for a single queen, who may live for two or three years and devote her entire life to laying eggs. A virtual egg-laying machine, she's capable of laying up to 3,000 eggs in a single day.

During summer, the worker bees are busy gathering nectar. They forage up to six miles from the hive, and it's estimated that to produce one pound of honey, bees visit two million flowers, travel an astonishing 55,000 miles, and make 75,000 trips back and forth to the hive.

Inside the hive, other workers concentrate the nectar into honey by adding enzymes and fanning the mixture to evaporate water content. On hot summer days, they also cool the hive by gathering in a corner near the entrance and fanning their wings to circulate the air. Everything the worker bees do is remarkably orderly and seemingly intelligent.

Then there are the drones, whose only contribution to the colony is to fertilize new queens. Like the queens, they cannot feed themselves, so during the summer, while the worker bees are busy gathering nectar and cooling the hive, the drones bask in the sun waiting to be fed.

When a new queen is ready to mate—an act that takes place high in the sky—the drones pursue her by the hundreds. Eventually she mates with about 18 of them, who die when fertilization is complete. The unsuccessful drones return to the colony to be fed more nectar and await the hatching of another queen.

Drones that last through the summer are doomed when the first frosty days of autumn arrive. With the mating season over, they're no longer needed, and the worker bees start guarding the hive entrance, refusing to let them in. I've often seen a worker bee dragging a reluctant drone out of the hive. Conserving energy is essential to the survival of the colony over winter, and there's no room for unproductive bees that would only consume valuable food reserves.

As days shorten and nights approach freezing temperatures, the bees prepare for winter by clustering in the center of the hive, where the huddle of thousands of bodies keeps the queen warm and even allows for hatching new eggs. The cluster is surrounded by honey gathered during the summer, which will nourish the bees during the long months ahead. As winter progresses, the colder bees on the outer part of the cluster rotate to the center, while the warmer bees get pushed to the outside, a strategic rotation that equalizes the bees' body temperature.

In Vermont, winters are long and cold, often lasting from November to late March, and temperatures can drop to twenty or thirty degrees below zero. It's a long time for a bee colony to survive and, indeed, many do not. During most of the year I keep my bees in the apple orchard, but when the first really cold days arrive, I bring the hives into my cellar, where the moist dirt floor helps to keep the temperature at a constant 45° F. So far, my bees thrive in this moderate environment, and when the first warm sunny days of late March arrive, they're ready to be moved back out to the orchard where they can begin harvesting nectar and pollen from early spring flowers.

During the coldest, darkest days of winter, I find joy and comfort in going down to the cellar where my bee hives stand on a wooden pallet. Pressing my ear against a wooden hive, I rap gently with my knuckles and hear a wonderful hum that lets me know my bees are alive and well. Pleased, I go back upstairs and settle into my comfortable chair by the woodstove, knowing that spring will return shortly, and we all will have survived another winter.

A colony that does survive can be a great honey producer, making as much as one hundred pounds or more over a summer. I began a recent year with three colonies, one that had overwintered in my cellar and the other two "package" bees that I'd purchased from an apiary in Georgia. I placed the three white hives at the back of my orchard against a stone wall that's nearly covered by shrubs. Every day I visited my little apiary, always looking at what the bees brought back to their hives. Sometimes it was pollen carried in hairy baskets on their legs to feed to young bees. Other times they brought nectar to make honey. Sometimes I couldn't help thinking that the bees just flew around for the fun of it.

In early spring I always watch to see what kinds of pollen the bees collect. Bees have a keen sense of smell and can locate flowering plants from miles away. I can tell which spring flowers are in bloom by the color of the pollen bees bring in long before I see the flowers themselves. The first pollen is always olive-colored, which I recognize as willow. Later, it's red or orange, indicating that it comes from wild spring beauties blooming in the woods or crocuses coming up in someone's garden.

Over the years, wild animals have left my bee hives alone, although occasionally skunks will bother them, scraping at the entrance and eating the bees that come out to protect the hive. The year before I got my new package bees, however, a hungry bear had gotten into my old hives, chewing honey from loaded frames and breaking the wooden boxes apart. I was so upset that I put up an electric fence and kept a careful lookout for the bear. I had no further problems that season, so when winter came I took down the fence and, not having seen a bear for some time, felt reasonably certain my bees would be safe the next spring. But when spring arrived, my son Tom warned me that I should put the fence up again or there'd be trouble. I agreed it was probably a reasonable precaution, but like lots of things I plan to do, I kept putting it off.

Every morning I looked from my bedroom window down into the orchard to enjoy the view of my three white hives standing against the shrub-covered stone wall. One morning in early July, I looked from the window to see all three hives scattered around the orchard, honey-laden frames smashed and boxes turned over in what looked like a war zone. I was devastated.

Putting on my bee suit and helmet, I began the nasty task of putting back together whatever could be salvaged. The bees were unhappy and ready to sting whatever came their way. I took ten stings on my exposed hands, and they even climbed up my pants to sting me on my legs.

I couldn't tell if any queens were still alive at first, but I noticed a cluster of bees clinging to a damaged frame. Looking closely, I saw they were surrounding a queen, distinguishable by her larger size. I carefully placed the cluster and queen in the least damaged hive. The other two colonies had lost their queen and, without an egg laying source, did not survive.

Now I had good reason to put up the electric fence to protect my one remaining hive. I bought a new battery for the fence charger and strung two strands of wire, spacing them so they would be at the right height for a bear's nose. I tested the wire with a blade of grass to be sure I could feel the numbing sensation that tells me the fence is working.

That evening I remembered something a seasoned beekeeper told me a long time ago: once a bear has found a hive, it will return the next day for more honey. At about nine o'clock, I decided to go out to the orchard to make sure the fence was doing its job. It was dusk when I headed out, and as I approached the hive, I saw a black shadow looming against the shrubby thicket along the wall. Then I saw it move—it was the biggest black bear I've ever seen, and it was just outside the fence by my last remaining bee hive. The bear and I stared at each other and I wondered which one of us would run first.

I finally shouted in as powerful a voice as I could muster, "Get out of here!" The bear turned and crashed through the shrubbery, over the stone wall, and into the hayfield beyond. It was the last I saw of the bear that year.

Beekeeping has taught me many lessons, and now I know from personal experience that when a bear has once feasted on honey, it is sure to return for more. I keep my electric fence up and charged throughout bee season now. My bees and I work too hard to give our honey away to a marauding freeloader.

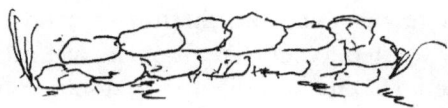

Stone Walls

I walk a mile up my road and back every day, in part to exercise the dogs I've had over the years, in part to exercise myself. Our road is named for the Schillhammer family who used to own the farm next door to mine. From my house, the road climbs gently uphill to the old Schillhammer farmhouse, and the length of dirt road between the two is lined with lichen-covered stone walls.

One of my dogs started me paying closer attention to these walls. She loved to chase the squirrels and chipmunks that use the walls for hiding places. The dog was fast, but the critters were faster, and they quickly scurried into hiding when they saw her coming. She never caught one, but she never quit trying.

After she'd sniffed and pawed at a hole where some squirrel or chipmunk had disappeared, she would jump up onto the wall and run effortlessly along the top. While I wondered at how she managed to place her feet solidly on the uneven stones, I started noticing the special workmanship that went into building these old walls.

Those that run past my house and extend on both sides of the road for the quarter mile up to the Schillhammer farm are among the most skillfully made walls I've seen. For some reason, they end right at the boundary, where suddenly the stones appear to have been simply tossed into rows with no attempt to build them into walls. The lengths I think of as mine are sturdy and attractive and have lasted for several generations, withstanding the effects of water, ice, weather, and time. They're a tribute to the early inhabitants of my land who gathered the stones from the fields, moved them to the roadside, and crafted them into such durable structures.

I can only imagine how many stones they had to contend with as they cleared the land they wanted to cultivate. It must have been a daunting task, first to cut the forest, then to dig up the stones—some of them quite sizable—and somehow manage to get them all delivered to the roadside. They had only themselves and their horses or oxen to work with, so the labor must have been backbreaking, but at least those early settlers could view their progress with satisfaction as they saw their fields cleared and their walls growing.

On my morning walks, I sometimes stop to study my walls. True to my calling, one of the first things I noticed is that they host five species of lichens and three species of moss. These small plants thrive on the moist surfaces of the stones, and the various compositions of the different stones favor one species over another. A common gray-green lichen called *Parmelia* dominates, brightening up and making the walls quite colorful after a rain. Most of the lichens grow, as *Parmelia* does, to form flat circular patches that don't seem to change much over the years. Actually, they are growing but so slowly it's hard to see any change. Patches six inches across are more than two hundred years old.

Next I turned my attention to how carefully the individual stones are arranged. Each seems to occupy a special place in the wall, and I got to wondering just how many there were in the stretch I walk past every morning. So I measured one ten-foot section, counted the stones, and did some math. I counted two hundred stones in the section, which meant that the walls that border both sides of the quarter-mile stretch of road between my house and the Schillhammer boundary hold upwards of 52,000 stones.

Most are roughly six to twelve inches in diameter, but some of the bigger ones are two feet across. Many are rounded, as if they'd been rolled along by the glaciers into oversize cobblestones. A rich assortment of rock types suggests they came from different areas far away from Schillhammer Road, each plucked from its distant bedrock and transported by passing glaciers to this part of Vermont.

It's hard for me to conceptualize how much physical labor went into gathering, moving, and arranging more than 52,000 stones that are part of my walls. My only experience with such labor was years ago when I decided to build a fieldstone fireplace in my house. As best I can remember, I collected about a thousand stones from a collapsed wall in the back pasture and hauled somewhere between twenty and thirty loads of them over to the house on an old stone boat—a kind of wooden skid or sled that farmers used to drag stones out of their fields when they were clearing land for planting. I pulled the sled with my tractor, but even with only a thousand stones to move and a tractor to help, I was exhausted, so I can appreciate how long and hard those early wall-builders must have worked.

While building my fireplace, I also learned that arranging stones requires skill, patience, and a strong back. Each stone in a wall or a fireplace has to fit precisely, which means a lot of trial and error. A stone mason once told me, "Every stone has its place so nothing is wasted," but that doesn't mean that finding the place is easy. Of course I built indoors and used mortar to hold my fireplace together, but I still had to select stones that fit next to one another. They also had to be flat in the right places, balanced in size, and attractive enough to serve as the side wall of my living room. So I had my own challenges that added a bit of complexity the outdoor wall-builders didn't have to worry about.

Still, they had to work harder and longer than I did, and their walls, even exposed to the elements, might well outlast my fireplace. With both the roadside walls and my fireplace so much a part of my daily life, I'm constantly reminded that the stones they're made of came along with the fertile, glacially derived soils that cover Vermont's landscape. And there seems to be an infinite supply of them. As one of my neighbors says, "After you think you've removed them all, they just grow back the next year."

The Boulder

In addition to the stone walls that border Schillhammer Road, I've noticed several random piles of stones scattered around neighborhood pastures and wondered what they're doing there. After observing where each was located and checking the surroundings, I realized that they stood where bedrock is close to the surface making the soil too thin to plow. The early farmers apparently heaved the stones into these piles to open a bit of additional land for grazing.

Then there's the huge solitary boulder in the middle of a Schillhammer hayfield that never made its way into a wall or a pile—it was just too big for human beings to move.

It's a massive stone, about twenty feet long, ten feet high, and it must weigh a hundred tons or more. Like most of the bedrock in our part of Vermont, it's what geologists call gray mica schist. Its surface is weathered, cracked, and worn. Clumps of moss grow in shady chinks, and tufts of grass struggle to survive in small pockets of soil, but gray and green lichens cover most of its surface. Except for its size and location, nothing about this boulder distinguishes it from lots of other sizable rock chunks—geologists call them glacial erratics—that the last glacier deposited around Vermont. But something about this particular boulder attracts people like a magnet.

The boulder is clearly visible from the road, and I've watched curious people stop their cars to stare at it or take pictures. I've had people knock on my door and ask permission to picnic beside it. Others let their children climb it and photograph them standing on top. In winter, I've seen both human and animal tracks leading from the road to the boulder and back, and recently a friend even reported tracks showing that a coyote had climbed to the top just as the children do. I don't know what mysterious force is at work here, but the boulder beckons, and people and animals alike respond.

On my daily walks, I've passed this boulder too many times to count, and I still wonder about its history. The last glacier, which covered Vermont under a mile-deep ice mass until about 12,000 years ago, must have delivered the stone to its current location. I can almost see it being carried slowly along in the massive ice sheet that sculptured our hills and valleys. But how did it get caught up in the glacier in the first place? Was it plucked from a cliff miles away—perhaps from Mt. Mansfield—and dragged to this field? Since glaciers move only a few inches a year, it would have taken more than a thousand years to move it a mile. If the massive boulder came from Mt. Mansfield, it embarked on a long journey indeed, taking at least 20,000 years to rest where it is now.

Unlike other stones still buried in the field, this boulder stands conspicuously on top of the glacial till. Outcrops of bedrock nearby show grooves, or what geologists call *striae*, that were made by materials dragged along at the bottom of the glacier. These striae provide ample evidence of the glacier's passing, but why did it deposit this one huge boulder on the surface right here? It's also fascinating to think that even before the glacier picked it up, the boulder had its own long history. It probably originated as rock that was part of the ancient Green Mountain Range, dating back some five hundred million years. In any event, the boulder I walk by every day is proof of major geological events that long predate human history.

I wonder what the early settlers who built the stone walls along Schillhammer Road thought about this immovable boulder? I can imagine generations of farmers mowing the field around it and hauling countless wagonloads of hay right by it. In the heat of summer, did they ever pause to rest in its shade? Did they perhaps lean against the cool stone? Did they wonder where this giant came from as I do? Did they know that it was deposited thousands of years ago by a glacier? Before the European settlers arrived, did Abenaki children climb the boulder the way children and coyotes do today? And what did the earliest European settlers who cleared the original forest think when they came upon this lone boulder in the wilderness?

All I know for sure is that these days the boulder is a prominent feature on my local landscape. It's perched on a hill in the middle of a wide open hayfield, a lone witness to huge geological processes and human history that's been lost to time. Its magnetic appeal makes me think of Stonehenge, but unlike Stonehenge, this one's natural and solitary. All it really is is a huge chunk of ancient rock, but by virtue of its size and solitary location it draws attention and fills those who see it with a sense of mystery and wonder.

My Neighbor Martha

Schillhammer Road makes a bend as it passes through the property that gave it its name—the Schillhammer family farm. At this bend is a tidy white farmhouse with green shutters and a slate roof. Behind the house there's a huge barn, long and gray with a slightly tipped silo at one end. Under the eaves on the front of the barn is a sign with faded white letters that reads "CRS Wilhelm Farm." I'm guessing that the "S" stands for Schillhammer, but I don't know who or what Wilhelm was. Behind the barn is an abandoned pasture now growing back to forest, and an old orchard with dying trees. Only a few of the old farm fields remain open. They're still mowed each year for the hay, which is sold to local equestrians to feed their horses.

When my family moved to Schillhammer Road in 1958, the old farm house was occupied by an elderly woman named Martha Fuller. She was the last of the most recent occupants, a group that included the owner, Carl Schillhammer, along with Martha's husband, Frank, and Frank's brother, Dewey, who worked as a hired man. Martha had served as the men's cook and housekeeper as long as they were alive, but since their deaths she'd lived alone where a once-prosperous dairy farm was already a fading memory.

Martha's old summer kitchen was attached to one end of the house, and it had a large cast-iron bell on its roof. A long cord attached to the bell hung down into the summer kitchen, and in the days of active farming Martha had pulled the cord at exactly 11:30 every morning to bring hungry farmhands in from the field to eat the midday meal she had prepared. The sharp clanging of the bell could be heard for miles around, and I've been told it originally hung at a fire station where it served as a town-wide alarm.

Martha once told me, "I don't like change," and indeed her house had not changed much either outwardly or inwardly since it was built in the 1840s. The place was like a time capsule that could have been a museum—it had all the trappings of a comfortable 19th century farmhouse. A black cast iron sink stood along a wall in the pantry, and wainscoting with heavy coats of green paint lined the kitchen walls. A single light with an ancient-looking green glass lampshade hung from the ceiling. I always enjoyed visiting Martha. The atmosphere in her home was warm and gave me a sense of well-being.

Martha was growing old when I knew her, but she had a full and pleasant face with sharp, smiling, blue eyes. She spent most of her days sitting in her kitchen in a wicker rocking chair near a window that faced the road. She had great eyesight—needing glasses only for reading—and when she wasn't reading she watched the world that passed by her kitchen window.

Every morning I walked my dogs a ways beyond Martha's house, and on the return trip I would stop to visit her. As I entered the kitchen, Martha always gave me a cheerful welcome and asked about the weather. It was always our first topic of conversation. I'd say, "Well, today it's cold and brisk," or, "It's blowing hard out there." She would nod and comment on the direction of the wind, for she was very observant. She sometimes remarked about the full moon and the wonderful shadows it cast on the meadow at night, and she often told me about deer she saw standing on the hill across the road.

Once she reported that while she sat on her front porch, a cow moose and calf had walked across the lawn only a few feet away. In spring and summer she often asked about the name of a wildflower she could see from the window, and on one visit she pointed out a tree at the edge of the orchard where a porcupine—she called it a hedgehog—was chewing away the bark. Every day she saw something new, which is one of the many things I liked about Martha.

One year she ordered a load of gravel to be spread on her driveway. I don't know where it came from, but shortly after it was delivered the driveway sprouted a variety of weeds. As a botanist, I was fascinated by the diversity of plant species that sprang up, many uncommon in Vermont. One in particular, a member of the pink family, was rare in our area. It was a small plant with dull green leaves and tiny white flowers that I showed to Martha because I suspected she'd be interested. She was delighted to learn about it and proudly showed her inconspicuous treasure to all visitors. She guarded this special flower carefully all summer, refusing to let anyone mow her weedy driveway.

Martha loved to garden, but she no longer had the strength to prepare her garden plot for planting. Nonetheless, she would spend late winter thinking about it, planning what vegetables she wanted, and ordering seeds from a mail order catalog. When the gardening season arrived, she would ask me sheepishly if I would plant them for her. I was pleased to work up the small patch behind her house where the soil was sandy and easy for Martha to weed. I'd plant the seeds she ordered, and once they were in the ground Martha would tend to her vegetables solicitously for the rest of the season.

Martha was a good friend, and I didn't mind helping her with various chores over the seasons. One of my greatest pleasures, in fact, was the year-round chore of splitting wood for her old-fashioned cook stove, which deserves a chapter of its own, coming up.

Splitting Martha's Wood

The dominant feature in Martha's kitchen, if not in her whole house, was the massive cast iron cook stove that stood along one wall. It had a huge black top with six griddles (or pot openings) and a reservoir for heating water. It had space enough to cook dinner for a large farm family, a purpose it served well for many years. A large oven door on the front of the stove had a broken catch that was held shut by a stick Martha braced between the floor and the door handle. I have no idea how long the catch had been broken, but I do know that countless pies and loaves of bread had been baked in this old oven, broken door or not.

A big black stovepipe emerged from the back of the stove and rose straight toward the ceiling until it made a sharp bend and disappeared into the wall. Martha feared a house fire, so every night she let the embers in the stove die out. In the morning she would start a new fire, piling dry wood into the firebox and pouring half a cup of kerosene over it, then lighting a match. Whoomph! And she had a fire.

This wood stove was at the center of Martha's life. Most of her day she spent only a few feet away from it, and she was never far from the wood box that she constantly drew upon to feed the fire. The stove burned winter and summer and was a source of heat both for the house and for cooking, but I guess best of all it was a warm friend. The large wood box that stood along the wall across from the stove needed regular filling, and that soon became my daily chore. After our morning greetings, I'd open the door to the woodshed attached to the house and stare at the great piles of wood that needed splitting.

It was neatly stacked in rows about four feet high—lots and lots of wood, at least five cords or more—enough to keep Martha's stove fired up all winter and spring, summer, and the next fall, as well. A local supplier delivered and stacked the firewood, which he'd cut into fifteen-inch lengths and split into quarters with a power splitter. The quarters were almost the right size to fit into the stove, but most had to be split once more so Martha, with a touch of arthritis in her hands, could manage them. Smaller logs, like the branches that didn't need splitting, Martha called "round wood."

A huge, gnarled chopping block cut from the trunk of a large tree stood in the center of the woodshed. The top was badly chewed by ax blows that had split hundreds of cords of wood over the years. The block was tough, though, and I never worried about needing a replacement. I tried to determine what kind of wood it was, but it was so badly shredded I couldn't tell. Even after all my years of chopping on it, it remained a mystery. The bark was gone and it had smooth sides and a ring of knobby protrusions—nothing to identify it, but it did have character, and must have caught the eye of some farmer long ago.

To split a length of wood to the proper size, I stood it upright on the chopping block and, with a swift stroke of the ax, I could pop the wood into two pieces—that is, if I struck it in just the right place. A little study beforehand, looking for slight cracks, helped me determine where the weak spots were located and I aimed for those. When I first started splitting Martha's wood, I was lucky to hit the end of the log anywhere at all, but after many years of practice I got so I could almost "split a hair."

Actually, learning to split Martha's wood wasn't as easy as I've made it sound. The woodshed had a low ceiling, which was challenging for someone my size—about five-foot-ten—but definitely taller than Martha. The ceiling was high enough that I could stand upright but too low for me to swing the ax over my head, so I had to modify my swing and still muster enough force to split the wood.

And then there was the bare light bulb that dangled directly above the chopping block.

Despite the low ceiling and dangling light bulb, though, I eventually managed to become a decent wood splitter and provided Martha with many a cord to feed her stove. In the process I learned a lot about wood, which has always fascinated me. I love its colors and textures, its feel and its smell.

Even the bark has character, and I've learned to recognize the different species of trees by the designs etched in their bark. Beech trees have smooth gray bark, while maple's bark is dark gray or black with strong, interlacing fissures. Black cherry has black bark that's checkered and sheds into small square plates, while white ash has gray bark with tight, shallow, parallel ridges.

Splitting wood has also taught me about the structural qualities of the wood. My spirits always rise when I see a piece of ash, knowing it will easily pop in two with just a light blow of my ax. And I dread hardhack that taxes my muscles and patience. As its name implies, it just doesn't want to split. Elm is a little like hardhack, tough and fibrous, and it only splits when there are no knots to hold it together.

I've learned to admire how trees have evolved, too. Their wood is strong with long fibers that are remarkably tough and resilient. Each species of tree has its own internal makeup, and I can now recognize the species by looking at the split side of a piece of firewood revealing the grain structure and color.

Sometimes I reflect on where the wood I'm splitting once grew and what extremes of weather it might have witnessed over the years. Did it survive ice storms and hurricanes as well as sugar snows and mild winters? I'm reminded of Martha, who herself had seen many extremes of weather in her long years. She told me about snowstorms when drifts reached halfway up the windows, and about hot, dry summers when water was scarce.

Some of these events are recorded clearly in the wood of local trees, and I can see them if I look closely—hot dry summers produce narrow tree rings, while wider rings indicate pleasanter, wetter seasons. Consistently wide and well-spaced rings might indicate that the tree grew in a favorable location, perhaps on a warm, south-facing slope where the soil was deep and moist. Consistently narrow and crowded rings suggest that the tree grew close by its neighbors and had to share the sunlight, moisture, and soil nutrients with them. Sometimes there's less growth on one side of a tree than on the other, indicating that a bigger tree may have grown close by, partly shading and slowing the growth on that side of its neighbor.

Even the branches of trees taught me things about how wood anatomy works. The lower portions produce extra wood, for instance, to give the branches the structural support they need to stretch far outward without breaking.

I learned from the wood of trees that had been used for sugaring, too. Once I split a piece of sugar maple and exposed an old tap hole that marked the place a small spout had fed maple sap into a bucket during spring sugaring season. The tap hole was covered over by several inches of new wood, but I could still see the marks of the drill that made the hole. By counting the growth rings of new wood, I could tell how many years ago the tap hole had been made.

Whenever Martha saw a piece of wood with a tap hole in it, she'd smile as it brought back pleasant memories of gathering sap in springtime and boiling it into syrup in the old sugarhouse in her maple woods, collapsed now for years.

Martha herself told me one last thing about wood. I always took the time to split enough wood to refill the box in her kitchen, which would give her what she needed to last another day. By the time I finished, she would already be starting to fuss with her pots, getting ready to prepare her midday meal. One day as I piled wood in her wood box, I came upon an ugly, twisted piece and asked if it would burn well. Always ready with an answer, Martha turned from her pots with a smile and said, "Crooked sticks make straight ashes."

Martha's Christmas Tree

M y neighbor Martha enjoyed good health but she eventually needed a walker to get around her house. Because her mailbox was some distance to walk, it was a challenge for her to get to it, so I started bringing in her mail and newspaper when I stopped by each morning to split wood.

Usually there wasn't much mail, maybe an advertising flyer or a bill. But on her birthday and during the Christmas season, she always received extra letters and cards that she greatly enjoyed. She'd count them carefully and tell me how many she received each year. Then she would read each one over and over again and show me her favorites.

Christmas was a special time of year for Martha, bringing back memories of happy times and the bustle of activity on the farm. Each year I'd find a small pine tree in a nearby field and cut it for her Christmas tree. She was always pleased but she never took it for granted. One year, when I told her it was time to cut the tree, she smiled with pleasure and said, "I was afraid you had forgot."

Knee-deep snow had fallen the night before my errand, but I managed to push through to a small tree that grew near the center of one field. Every year I mow that field for hay and I'd watched the tiny pine grow, always taking care to mow around it, waiting for it to be ready. By that December, it was tall enough to be called a Christmas tree. It was a handsome white pine with soft green needles, and I almost hated to cut it down, but when I remembered it was for Martha I decided it was perfect.

I dragged the tree back up to her house, nailed it to a homemade tree stand, and pulled it into her kitchen. Martha exclaimed at how nice it looked and wondered where I got it. I explained it was growing near a rock in the hay field below the red barn, and she seemed to know the exact spot. When I stood the tree up, it brushed the kitchen ceiling, so I had to take it out and cut a foot off the bottom. I brought it back and placed it in a corner to let Martha look it over. "Yes," she pronounced, "it's a fine looking tree."

The next morning I walked up the hill as usual to attend to chores and enjoy our daily visit. Under the Christmas tree, Martha had arranged a display of toy sleighs and a basket full of teddy bears and dolls. She'd managed to hang a few ornaments from the tree's branches, but it still needed decoration. Martha said she had trouble reaching the upper branches, so I obliged by hanging some bright red ornaments to complement the golden angels she'd hung lower down.

She asked about my own Christmas tree, and I told her we were just getting ready to look for one. Marie thought it would be nice to have a balsam fir this year rather than one of the white pines we had year after year, but I knew finding a fir would be a challenge. White pines grow everywhere in the abandoned fields around our neighborhood, but balsam firs are hard to come by.

With a distant look in her eye, Martha told me about two fir trees that once grew near her old sugarhouse. She thought perhaps some young ones might be growing there now. The sugarhouse had collapsed years ago and there was no trace where it once stood, but sugaring in the spring had always been the best of times for Martha and remained an important reference point in her life.

By then, the snow was already too deep for me to search for new fir trees that might not even be there, but I said nothing about that to Martha. I figured that this year might be the first time in a very long time that I would have to buy a Christmas tree. But that was none of Martha's worry.

I left her admiring her tree and went into the shed to split some wood. When I came back to the warm kitchen, I heard the tinkling of a music box playing "Santa Claus Is Coming to Town." In the middle of the kitchen table, Martha had placed a tiny red Santa that turned slowly in a circle while the music box inside played its Christmas tune.

I wondered if this was a new Christmas gift but Martha said no, it had been given to her brother-in-law, Dewey, the Christmas before he died.

Martha smiled and the music slowed. She commented that it didn't play for very long, so I picked it up, rewound it, and put it back on the table to play some more. When I turned around, Martha was standing by her Christmas tree with all her favorite toys lying at its base and her special Christmas music playing in the background, quietly smiling.

Martha's Ghosts

"I hear voices. This house is haunted."

Martha made the announcement when she figured she had known me long enough to trust me with this secret.

Her pronouncement surprised me. I had always found Martha a steady, cheerful, reliable, no-nonsense person, not prone to fantasies. And the Schillhammer house had never looked or felt the least bit haunted to me.

Everything I knew about Martha argued against the possibility of mental decline. She was alert, articulate, intelligent, and still a reader of books, newspapers, and magazines. She had been the town librarian, still enjoyed good eyesight, and often read for five or six hours in a day. She was especially fond of clever mysteries that could be solved by rational means. I knew my morning visits had become an important part of Martha's daily rhythms and I suspected the secret she'd been keeping had weighed heavily on her mind while we were getting to know each other, so I gave her my full attention now.

She was seated in her usual rocking chair near the wood stove, and I noticed that she looked worried. She began by explaining that what she was telling me was personal. She couldn't confide in anyone else, she said, because they would think she was crazy. I listened carefully as she described the voices she heard coming from her basement. A man's deep voice would talk and sing and there was dancing. She'd hear the voices coming up through the floor register at the foot of her chair, and she'd stack books and magazines on top of the register to deaden the sound.

She went on to say that sometimes a voice also came from the television set, and she would pull the plug to stop it. I'd wondered why her television was unplugged some mornings but had never asked, even though it posed a special challenge for me when I had to look up the codes to get it operating for her again.

I tried to comfort her by telling her how strange noises sometimes happen with modern equipment. Her telephone line might be picking up radio waves that were the source of the voices. To reassure her, I bought a small electronic box designed to provide better phone reception and added it to her line. I thought that if the voices were in her head, the box might persuade her that they weren't there anymore, but she continued to hear them, now reporting multiple voices. She said a whole family was in the cellar.

Martha continued to hear these voices quite regularly, which concerned me, but I never heard anything myself. She said I never would because when I was in the house the voices stopped. So she went on living with her ghosts, and I continued my daily visits, hoping the voices wouldn't get to be too much for her.

Eventually I bought the Schillhammer farm from Martha, and she continued to live in the house until she died. I was sad to lose my friend, but I decided that the best use for her wonderful old farmhouse was to rent it to people who would enjoy living in the country. I had it renovated to make it more livable for modern tenants and soon rented it to a friendly couple from Colorado. Ed worked for IBM, and he and his wife, Judy, wanted to live in the country where they could have a garden and Ed could ride his horse on weekends. During the two years they lived in Martha's house, neither of them ever heard the voices, or at least they never reported them to me. But they were a proud professional couple and not the sort to complain that the house was haunted, even if it was.

My next tenants, Steve and Barbie, came from Alaska to start a new life in Vermont. Steve was friendly but quiet, and Barbie was outgoing, energetic, maybe even a bit eccentric. One day I saw her standing in the hayfield behind the house wearing a huge straw hat and flying a kite. I liked her spirit and unconventional ways.

After they'd lived there for a while, Barbie came to me, excited, and announced, "The house is haunted! Voices are coming from the cellar!"

She described a man's deep voice, but she couldn't make out what he was saying, except that he clearly referred to someone named Max. The man talked and sang and made the dishes rattle in the kitchen. I told Barbie that her description fit with Martha's, and she was delighted to think that the house was indeed haunted. She claimed to have an unusual sense of the supernatural and assured me that the ghosts in Martha's old farmhouse were good ghosts.

I was curious about Barbie's reference to Max, so I called Martha's sister, Rose, to ask if she knew anyone by that name.

"Max was our father's name and also our brother's," she said. Rose added that on weekends the whole family would gather at the house to cook, talk, play music, and dance. I found myself beginning to wonder.

After two years, Steve and Barbie moved to southern Vermont, and at that point I sold the Schillhammer house to my son Tom, who moved in with his wife, Mary. They knew about the haunted house stories, but they never heard voices, which didn't surprise me. They're both scientists.

Then, during a college break, their daughter Alice came to visit. Alice said she heard strange sounds in the house and dishes rattling in the kitchen. One night she was awakened by the sound of a woman singing on what sounded like a scratchy old gramophone recording. Alice thought someone might have left the television on, but when she went to the TV room no one was there and the television was off. On yet another occasion when Alice was alone in the house, she heard distinct heavy footsteps, like a man's, in the room overhead.

Alice's older brother, Scott, had his own extraordinary experience during a visit there. Scott had placed his knapsack and other belongings in a corner of his room before going to bed. Late that night, he suddenly awakened to see a man crouched over his gear. According to Scott, the man noticed that he was awake, then stood up, walked away, and disappeared into the wall!

Both Scott and Alice are mature and well-educated, and neither had been the kind of young person who believed in ghosts or haunted houses. I now found myself wondering in earnest what the chances were that a woman who had just arrived from Alaska could come up with the same tales that Martha told. Or the name Max. And what were the chances that two rational young people—my own grandchildren—could imagine voices and visible ghosts? As a scientist, I never believed that there were such things as haunted houses, but I now admit, I'm not so sure.

III.
Writing through
a Natural Year

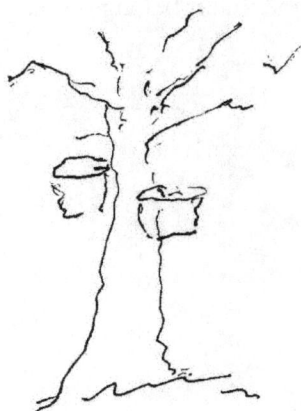

My dear friend Mary Jane Dickerson wrote a wonderful poem to surprise me at a dinner in 2006 celebrating an honorary degree bestowed upon me by the University of Vermont. Mary Jane entitled it "Vermont's Man For All Seasons," and she somehow managed to capture most of what I had been writing about since my retirement.

As Mary Jane indicates in her poem, I spend much of my time outdoors, sometimes busy at tasks but sometimes just wandering around wondering about things and marveling at my good fortune to have found such a perfect place to live. Because I am outdoors so much, I notice the seasons coming and going, changing and evolving, repeating themselves and occasionally surprising me with something I hadn't noticed or thought about before.

The essays that follow represent my effort to write my way through a natural year. I begin with Mary Jane's poem because it strikes me that it belongs here. — H. V.

MORE: But, Richard, in office they offer you all sorts of
things. I was once offered a whole village, with a mill and
a manor house, and heaven knows what else—a coat of
arms, I shouldn't be surprised. Why not be a teacher?
You'd be a fine teacher. Perhaps even a great one.

RICH: And if I was, who would know it?

MORE: You, your pupils, your friends, God. Not a bad
public, that . . .Oh, and a quiet life.

Robert Bolt, A Man For All Seasons (1960)

Vermont's Man for all Seasons

(for Hub Vogelmann, April 29, 2006)

This man for all seasons, Hub
Vogelmann, teacher, scientist
and one for the quiet life,
reads landscapes the way
most people read books,
always placing his trust
in nature's script, not
in those pages inscribed
by the rest of us.

His eyes, eagle-sharp, scan
the open field, catching the coyote and her pup
nosing along the woods' edge, the deer
grazing by the lower stone wall,
the wood duck leading ten ducklings
across the pond toward the sheltering grasses,
a moose family on its way to the Winooski,
stopping to forage as they move along,
stopping to turn their deep eyes

toward the lighted window
where another family seat
themselves around the table.

Each day, from the depths of winter's frozen hush
through a spectrum of spring greens
into the lush growth of a Vermont summer
and sweet autumn's ripeness,
this man for all seasons reads
the news from Schillhammer Road
during his two mile walk, news
writ large in tracks criss-crossing
early morning's snowfall, all year long
in cans and bottles he picks up, in spring
the news unfurling as an ongoing drama
of twelve species of ferns, their lacy
sprays opening into green spires
throughout the low lying expectant woodland
with their likely and their unlikely names,
"Interrupted," "Cinnamon," "Hayscented,"
"Ostrich," "Sensitive," "Bracken" and "Ladyfern."
Red maples flowering in April, a profusion
of male and female, patterned
in delicately wrought florets he deciphers
anew each year, delighting in this exuberant
evidence of the sex life of trees,
Amelanchier spreading its blossoms
near the wild apple trees,
and Colt's Foot beginning to thrust
its hardy shoots through roadside gravel.

This man for all seasons knows
how to feed off the land, tracking
his own wild edibles the way most
bend and stoop to gather what grows
in their garden rows: in early spring,
day lily shoots near at hand, then

wild leeks waving their flattened leaves
like tiny banners in the breeze and fiddle heads
burgeoning, coiled like taut green springs
embedded in the alluvial soil
along the Winooski's banks,
Lamb's Quarters in disturbed soil
and succulent morels in season.
Then, when the softening soil
signals its warm readiness, this man,
a creator of his own dream of utopia,
plants and tends his spot of this earth,
vegetables lovingly domesticated
under his knowing hand, abundant potatoes
of every shape and hue, peas and beans reaching toward
the sun, the crucifers he shares with four-footed visitors,
tomatoes reddening into July, squashes and cucumbers
fecund under their umbrella leaves, pumpkins turning
from flecked greens into burnt orange as day length
changes,
spilling their fruits into the surrounding fields.
This man whose profile, as time passes,
more and more resembles the rugged peaks
of Camels Hump, that Vermont landscape
he has made his own, a terrain
forever bearing his imprint, there
meticulously reading the lessons learned
from dying red spruce—what we yet struggle
to understand for our own survival—
showing generations of students the care needed
for its sub-arctic plants, this mountain
a fragile ecosystem crowning Vermont.

From his early pursuit of the primrose in Utah,
earning the sobriquet "Flower Doctor,"
and study of plants in the sub-arctic
with Marie at his side, both swatting,
finally enduring dense swarms of black flies, to summers

away in Colombia collecting medicinal plants
and seeing what he could read in fog's
condensation in Mexico's cloud forests,
then to eventual invitations far and wide
to lecture on acid rain or Arctic plants,
sometimes in a painful Spanish, yet
always he returned, year in and year out, carrying on
his methodical work with Vermont's mountains,
running up and down Camels Hump
to observe and then record
what this venerable place reveals
about what's happening to all living things.

This man for all seasons, this man of his times,
wherever he roamed, always yearned toward
Schillhammer Road—the quiet life there he shared
with Marie, their three sons, Tom, Jim and Andy.
Rooted as deeply as the ancient maples
shading the house and lining the road,
he came home to the beehives in the orchard,
wintering them in the cellar, tapping on the wooden hives
for their answering buzz, in summer
chasing marauding bears away from the lure of honey,
scratching the Black Angus bull's back with a garden rake,
fishing his Sundays away for Pike, Shad or Yellow Perch
on Shelburne Pond, drilling holes through the ice
on Lake Champlain's Keeler Bay, greeted
at the door by Marie with "You
always smell like a cow or a fish."
Walking the dogs along Schillhammer Road,
he pauses and hunkers down to study the wooly bear
as it inches its way south at early hints of autumn's chill,
then returns to sit on the back veranda
where he can survey his domain
and feed red squirrels, chipmunks, a white weasel
on occasion and birds in all seasons,

his porch a haven for those who sense
they are being fed by one of their own
even if he is a two legged creature, this man,
with his care for the land and all it yields,
shows what its rewards might be
if we could read all it has to say, this man
for all seasons, like Voltaire's wise Dr. Pangloss,
inspires us to know ourselves and our place
in the nature of things so we too might learn
to "cultivate our garden," enriching our own lives
and those of others who share this planet Earth.

Mary Jane Dickerson
April 29, 2006

Spring Begins in January

The calendar says that spring begins on March 21, the spring equinox, with twelve hours of daylight and twelve hours of darkness.

The equinox may be an important celestial event, but it's not when spring begins. The real spring—biological spring—begins here in Vermont during late January. All you have to do is watch the natural world to see the earliest signs of it.

At the approach of winter, the days become shorter and temperatures drop. It's a time when all living things make their own special arrangements to survive the cold months ahead. Plants die or go into dormancy. Deciduous trees shed their leaves, and the aboveground parts become physiologically hardened in preparation for the freezing days to come. Some animals migrate or hibernate, while others settle into a restless sleep. Some that remain active burrow into or tunnel through the snow to hide themselves from owls and other hungry predators. A quiet loneliness settles over the landscape as the biological activities of summer and fall give way to winter's chill darkness. Each species, whether it's active or inactive during the winter, lives for the time when it can begin a new biological cycle come spring.

The first signs of spring's awakenings begin to show as the days lengthen after the winter solstice. December 21, the shortest day of the year, has only nine hours and four minutes of daylight and fourteen hours and fifty-six minutes of darkness. In the middle of that longest night of the year, it can seem as if the sun might never rise again, but after the first of January the sun comes up a little earlier and sets a little later every day. It's a gradual but welcome change, and all life is grateful that the winter solstice—the darkest time of winter—is now behind us.

Even though the early changes are slow, the days continue to lengthen, and soon one more minute of daylight is added to each passing day. By January 21 the day length has reached nine hours and thirty-five minutes—not much more than we had on December 21, but it's enough to cause a stir in the natural world.

Chickadees now whistle their two-note territorial song, and some woodpeckers drum away at dead tree limbs as if they're dress-rehearsing for the mating season that will arrive soon. Crows that had drifted south in the fall begin to reappear, and their raucous caws are a welcome sound. Cardinals sing clear, sweet songs that can be heard from a considerable distance, and house finches perched in tree tops sing more insistently now.

Even dormant plants begin to show the earliest signs of new life. Tree buds and young twigs begin to display a bit of color as the longer days cause pigments to form. When the sun shines, a soft, warm hue shows in the tree tops. The slender branches of a willow turn yellow and ochre, while the buds of maples shift toward light red. The stems of the shrubby dogwood called red-osier take on a deep reddish-purple that intensifies with each passing week.

Cold is no longer the determining factor in this natural landscape. It is light—the extra daylight—that triggers a biological spring. And it's exciting to watch it happen.

No matter how cold the days, and we suffer some of the coldest days in late January and early February in our part of the world, the temperature cannot alter the forces that are now set in motion. During the winter months, icicles form on the eaves of our houses and hang from rock ledges along the Interstate. The natural world remains frozen, but with the increasing strength of the sun each day brings the possibility of melting and a gradual shrinking of snow and ice cover.

Many years we even enjoy a January thaw about this time, when the melt accelerates for a few days. Dirt roads that dip slightly to the south absorb the most sun and begin to soften, sending rivulets of water trickling along their edges. Then the thaw passes, and we return to the deep freeze a while longer, but the increasing radiation and all that energy flowing from the sun for longer stretches each day is making it known to the natural world that spring is on its way.

Snow in February

A February snowstorm can feel like a setback, but David Ludlum's *Vermont Weather Book* confirms my observation that the natural world turns a corner during the January 20's.

Ludlum says, "The 'turn of winter' comes about January 26... with a gradual increase in the normal mean temperature following day by day." And my almanac tells me that during the short month that follows, day length will increase by just over seventy minutes. Because I know spring is coming, I can actually enjoy a snow that falls in February.

One recent February day, snow started to fall during the afternoon and continued through the night. When I woke up the next morning, the land around my house was covered with a soft white blanket that measured ten inches deep, enough to cover the brown grasses in my hayfield and hide all the dead vegetation that had been exposed during a January thaw. Overnight the landscape had been transformed into a fresh new world.

The bright February sun made the fresh snow glisten, crystalline flakes reflecting thousands of tiny lights as the sun's rays reached ground. Shadows cast on the snow made sharp, clearly-focused designs against the white background. The snowscape continued to change day by day. Wind sculpted surface patterns that looked like rippling ocean water and created drifts with sharp, curving edges and shelves. It blew up against a tree near my house and swirled and scoured the snow from around the trunk, leaving a well at the base of the tree.

Seeing the tree from a distance, I noticed that snow stuck to the upper sides of its branches creating what looked like a skeleton of the tree's crown. The dark underside of the branches reached outward from the trunk like brittle bones. But, when I went outdoors after dark, the contrasts of light and dark were obscured, and the soft white snow showcased the shape of the tree's crown without the distraction of that skeleton.

This past February, I welcomed snow that gave me a fresh look at the tracks of otherwise invisible nighttime visitors around my house. When I look closely at the tracks, I can tell who made them, where they came from, and where they went. Over the years I've seen evidence of deer, moose, rabbits, squirrels, mice, coyotes, foxes, and bobcats. If I follow some of the small mammal tracks, I sometimes see tracks where a larger predator pounced on its prey.

Some small critters such as field mice regularly travel under the snow, and I can see ridges marking their tunnels in the hayfield. Later, when the snow begins to melt, the remnants of these tunnels will reveal just how busy the field mice were scurrying around under protective cover. If the snow is deep enough—ten inches or more—another animal also uses it for cover. The ruffed grouse sometimes dives right into the deep snow and burrows a short distance from the entrance hole to hide from predators.

In fact, snow provides not only cover but warmth. During spells of low temperature, ruffed grouse sometimes stay in their snow burrows for several days at a time, emerging only at dawn and dusk to feed. Plants also benefit from this insulation. Soil temperatures under a blanket of snow are often above freezing, regardless of the temperature of the air outside. Studies have shown that the roots of plants continue to grow slowly during the winter, so there's lots of life under a February snow just waiting to activate when it disappears.

As winter finally gives way to spring, whatever late snows fall in February and even March will offer one last gift as they melt. The meltwater will slowly percolate down through the soil, starting life moving and growing again and winding up in the groundwater that supplies my well and enables me to enjoy a cold, clear glass of water.

Making Maple Syrup

Toward the end of February or early in March, when the sun is warm enough to produce daytime temperatures above freezing, it's sugaring time. That's when Vermonters tap their maple trees to make syrup.

All along Schillhammer Road, sap buckets hang from the big maple trunks. One of my neighbors taps most of our roadside trees every year, but I've reserved the three that are closest to my house for my own modest sugaring operation.

When temperatures are right—above freezing during the day but below freezing overnight—I drill about two inches deep through the bark of my maples into the sapwood that carries the tree's sweet liquid. I then tap a metal spout into the hole and hang a bucket on it to catch the sap that will soon drip from the spout. Once it begins to flow, I hear a steady drip, drip, drip throughout the day, and sometimes I even hear it at night when I step outdoors after dark. A good sap flow will fill a bucket in a day.

This period of sap flow depends on the alternating temperatures of early spring. During cold nights, a tree's roots draw water out of the soil and move it up the trunk into the branches overhead. But in the warmer daytime, the sap returns to the ground, and some of it flows out through my spouts and into the buckets. I hang three buckets on each of my three big maples and collect enough sap to supply my family and friends with sufficient syrup to carry us through until the next spring.

My sugaring operation is primitive. Long ago I built a hearth from bricks taken from a collapsing smokehouse on the Schillhammer farm, and each year when I'm ready to boil my sap down to syrup I place a large galvanized washtub on top of this hearth. At the end of each day I pour all the sap from my buckets into the tub, rehang the empty buckets on the trees, and light a fire under the tub using branches that have fallen during the winter. In the old days, I also burned scrap wood from the renovation of our 200-year-old farmhouse.

I let the sap simmer on the fire overnight, and in the morning I pour the much-reduced liquid into a smaller pan that I can boil on my kitchen stove until it reaches the thickness that I like for syrup. I have to watch carefully during this final stage so the sap doesn't boil over or lose too much water and caramelize.

The lightest colored syrup, which takes a lot of special handling, used to be called "Grade A Fancy," but these days it's called "Grade A Light Amber" or "Vermont Fancy." Serious sugarmakers try hard to produce great quantities of this top grade syrup—it brings the highest price—but my syrup is usually darker. Because I don't sell it, I don't grade it, but I'd guess the best of it might qualify as "Grade A Dark Amber," and most of the rest is probably Grade B. Toward the end of the season I sometimes even produce the darkest syrup of all—Grade C, considered nontable grade, or not "commercial." I don't worry a lot about what grade I get. I actually prefer the stronger maple flavor of darker syrup.

After I took up sugaring, I began to think of my three big maples as special friends. They not only produced delicious syrup each spring but provided shade in the summer and bore bright red and orange leaves in the fall. When one of these trees died, I felt as if I had lost an old and valued companion. I had trouble thinking about chopping it up for firewood and burning it, so I decided to have it milled into two-inch planks and I built a sturdy table with it that still stands in my kitchen. At breakfast each morning, I sit at this table and am reminded of the great tree it came from.

I'm fortunate to live in the part of the world where sugar maples grow. They're a dominant tree in the forests of the Northeast but are limited in their southward distribution. They need freezing weather to break seed dormancy. I'm concerned that global warming will cause a slow northern migration of maples that will result in a major change in the composition of our Vermont forests. Indeed, during the fifty years that I've been sugaring here, I've already observed that a warming climate has caused my first tapping date to move up about a week. Trees I once tapped during the first week of March, I'm now tapping in late February.

Maple sugaring is a grand tradition here in Vermont. It provides enjoyment and financial reward to farmers who have extra time available in early spring. For me it brings something more. It reminds me of the kinds of questions that drew me to science in the first place. As a botanist, I find the unknown factors affecting the movement of sap inside maple trees fascinating and am once again reminded of how little we scientists really know.

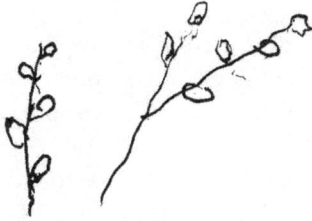

Pussy Willows

It's March 21, and I just saw my first pussy willows. They were growing in a low, swampy depression along Schillhammer Road.

They were a wonderful sight, for they mean that spring is gaining momentum. Although this is the first time I've seen pussy willows this year, I knew from watching my bees carrying their pollen that somewhere in the neighborhood pussy willows were further along.

As the days grow longer and the temperatures get warmer, willows end their dormancy and begin their new year. They're the first spring plants to flower—well ahead of most other flowering plants, which are still sleeping. Indeed, pussy willows are so anxious to start their new growth that they often flower while there's still snow on the ground.

There is something about pussy willows that brings a smile to people's face. Everyone seems to recognize them as a sign of spring, and I've never met a person who couldn't identify them when their buds are open. I treat pussy willows as fuzzy friends and bring branches into my house every March to remind me that shortly I'll be able to plant my garden. One year I found myself so impressed by one particular branch that I got out my oil paints and painted a picture of it. It was a simple portrait, a lone branch against a background of gray sky, but I liked it and hung it in the upstairs bathroom. Later, one of my houseguests told me it looked so real that she had to touch one of the "pussies" to make sure it was only a painting.

Those familiar silvery "pussies" are the pussy willow's male catkins. They are made of numerous male flowers that will shortly produce pollen and release it to the local winds. The less familiar female flowers grow on other trees and are so drab and inconspicuous that no one notices them. They are best seen after they've been pollinated, and the long-beaked capsules of their fertilized flowers have split open to disperse their seeds.

Pussy willows prefer to grow in wet soil, often in marshes or along stream banks, but they can do well in drier soils, as well. They have an extensive intertwining root system that makes them well-suited to control erosion. They also may be a good indicator of a high water table or subsurface water movement. Many years ago, when I wanted to dig a trout pond, I used pussy willows to lead me to a possible pond site. And sure enough, when the bulldozer began to dig into the soil, water rushed to the surface and filled the hole.

Pussy willows are not only a good indicator of water, they have a history of medicinal use as well. The inner bark contains salicin, which is used in over-the-counter painkillers like aspirin. Early American Indians extracted this compound from the bark and roots and used it to relieve pain and reduce fever. They also stripped the fibrous bark to make rope and weave it into baskets.

They're good at lightening people's mood, too.

One cold, snowy March day, I had a doctor's appointment and I arrived at the office with several branches of pussy willow that I gave to the receptionist. She broke into a big smile. "Pussy willows! What a wonderful surprise! Spring must really be here," she said, and treated them like they were rare orchids.

A clump of pussy willows still grows near that trout pond, and I gather a few of their branches every spring to share with family and friends. Pussy willows boost everyone's sun-deprived spirits and nourish our hope that winter is finally coming to an end.

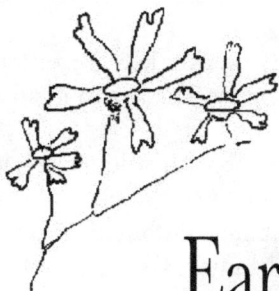

Early Spring Edibles

Winters are long in Vermont and by the time the snow melts I'm definitely looking forward to gardening again and eating all the fresh, green vegetables I'm going to grow. Actually, I can start eating fresh greens well before my garden starts producing them, but I have to be attentive to weeds and woodland plants.

The first of my early spring edibles appears just as the snow begins to melt, exposing the soil around the edges of my garden. I watch closely for the green leaves of a garden weed called *winter cress*. It grows in dense rosettes that were formed late during the preceding fall and are ready to start growing as soon as the snow disappears. Winter cress leaves are dark green and glossy with rounded lobes that make them look a bit like field mustard, which has smaller leaves, though, and does not show up this early in the spring.

I gather the cress leaves early, while it's still cold outside, because when the temperature warms they turn bitter. Young winter cress leaves taste somewhat like broccoli—a relative—and can be used as fresh salad greens or steamed and served as a hot vegetable. When winter cress begins to flower, I also pick the unopened flower heads, which look like miniature broccolis, and steam them for another delicious hot vegetable.

I have to wander away from the garden into the woods, or even down to the Winooski River, for my next spring edibles. In mid-April, wild leeks appear in rich, moist woodlands, including both wooded hillside slopes and floodplain forests. They're related to chives, onions, and garlic, all of which belong to the genus *Allium* and have a strong oniony aroma. Because various other early spring leaves can look as fresh and delicious as wild leeks, the oniony smell is key to identifying them.

One plant that people sometimes confuse with wild leeks goes by the common name *false hellebore*, and this one can be life threatening. It sometimes is mistakenly called skunk cabbage but unlike leeks it has broad heavily ribbed and pleated leaves. Many years ago, a secretary from the University of Vermont went trout fishing with some friends and ate some false hellebore that was growing near the trout stream. She immediately felt faint, couldn't walk, and had to be carried out of the woods to a waiting ambulance that one of her friends had rushed out to call.

False hellebore contains a powerful compound that can depress blood pressure to a dangerous low. Indeed, a few days after the incident with the secretary, I read about a group of fishermen in New Hampshire who made the same mistake, and one member of that group died.

In fact, searching for an effective blood pressure medicine, several pharmaceutical companies contacted me to ask if I could direct them to a good source of false hellebore. One company did manage to isolate the drug, which was marketed for a short time, but they eventually dropped it in favor of more effective treatments that came along.

For foragers on the hunt for wild edibles, remember that wild leeks have a distinctive onion aroma and false hellebore does not.

The leaves of wild leeks can be eaten raw, but they're strong tasting. I prefer to steam them as I would fresh spinach and serve them with butter. They also make a great potato-leek soup, which has a delicate flavor and is a great favorite with spring dinner guests. You can also eat the bulbs, but you may have to dig five or six inches into the soil to unearth them. Wild leeks have contractile roots that pull the bulbs a little deeper every year until they flower.

When flowering trees begin to bloom in early May, it's time to look for fiddleheads. Fiddleheads are the new young fronds of a common Vermont fern called the *ostrich fern*. Each fern produces a cluster of four or five tightly coiled fronds during the early weeks of spring, and Vermonters who don't eat any other wild foods often buy fiddleheads picked by local enthusiasts or even order them as expensive delicacies at gourmet restaurants.

The ostrich ferns grow abundantly in the floodplain bordering the Winooski River, thriving in the fine rich silt deposited anew by high water each spring. My search for the biggest and fattest of fiddleheads can be challenging because the Winooski's floodplain is often muddy, covered by standing pools of water, or littered with debris such as logs and brush left behind by spring floods. I've also found fiddleheads growing at the lower end of my hayfield where, over the years, erosion has deposited a deep bed of fine soil, and if the Winooski's floodplain is too messy, I take these.

Harvesting the fiddleheads is easy. You just break the crisp, emerald-green coils off the thick rootstock and throw them into a bag. Cleaning them is more of a challenge. The papery brown scales that protect the coiled fronds are stubbornly attached. I first empty my fiddleheads onto a coarse wire screen and blast them with a garden hose, stripping most of the scales off along with unwanted dirt. Then I rinse them further in the kitchen sink and eat them just as they are, toss them into a salad, or steam them for a few minutes. Steamed, they're especially tasty served chilled with a little vinegar and sprinkled with bacon chips. I like fiddleheads so much that I sometimes blanch and freeze them for a treat the next winter.

I continue to enjoy wild edibles throughout the growing season— young day lily leaves, lamb's-quarters, pigweeds, Jerusalem artichokes, wild elderberries, mushrooms, and more—but the earliest spring edibles are the ones I appreciate most. They announce the end of winter.

Shadbush

The first week of May typically brings with it the delicate white blossoms of a flowering tree called *shadbush*. Early New England settlers named this tree for the ocean-dwelling fish called shad, which they saw swimming up coastal rivers to spawn when shadbush was in bloom. The flowers appear before other trees have leafed out, and they're a welcome sight on a landscape that is still recovering from winter. They catch my eye immediately as they appear along roadsides, in fencerows, and among the leafless trees on wooded hillsides.

Shadbush is a small tree—or a tall shrub—that seldom reaches over thirty feet in height. The trunks or stems often grow in clumps, and even the larger specimens may look more like overgrown bushes than trees. Shadbush belongs to the rose family. It produces small red fruits that have earned it two of its other common names: *serviceberry* associates the time of its flowering with an old legend. According to the story, people who lived where the ground froze in winter watched for what they called serviceberry to bloom. The flowers meant that it would now be possible to dig a grave and hold a burial service for anyone who had died during the winter. Another name, *juneberry*, refers to the time when fruits appear. They ripen in June and can be harvested to make a delicious jelly—if you're fast enough. It's hard to find enough fruit left on the trees because they're a favorite food for several species of birds, including flocks of cedar waxwings who can clean a tree in minutes.

The early-flowering shadbush tree has become a seasonal indicator for many things. While settlers used shadbush to tell them shad were moving up the rivers, I use it to tell me that if I'm not already picking fiddleheads, I should get to it. It also tells me to look for an array of wildflowers such as spring beauty, dogtooth violet, and red trillium, which appear in response to the same seasonal cues that have started the more visible shadbush blooming. And if that's not enough, it also tells me to start looking for the return of tree swallows and orioles.

There are two common species of shadbush in our area, and they look much alike. They also grow near each other and flower at about the same time, so it takes a sharp eye to distinguish between them. One way to tell the difference is to pay attention to their timing: one species, *Amelanchier arborea*, flowers at about the same time its leaves begin to emerge, while the other species, *Amelanchier laevis*, flowers after the leaves are about half grown. Another way to tell them apart is to look at the undersides of their leaves: the young leaves of *A. arborea* are covered with fuzzy white hairs, while the underside of the leaves of *A. laevis* are smooth and shiny.

There is another shadbush, *Amelanchier bartramiana*, that grows in the subarctic and extends southward in the mountains all the way to New England. Named after the early American botanist William Bartram, it's a low bush that produces only a few inconspicuous white flowers in early summer. Most people who hike in Vermont's mountains walk right by it, not recognizing it as close kin to the commoner species that we use as seasonal indicators in the valleys below.

The first week in May is indeed a special time of year, when it seems that all of nature's forces are gathering momentum to rejuvenate the landscape. It will soon be a green world again, and people's outlook on life will be greatly improved. The burst of leaves on maples and other trees will soon overwhelm the modest shadbush, which, without its flowers, will fade into the background until another spring arrives.

Spectrum of Greens

A fter shadbush blooms, the spectrum of greens begins. The early spring landscape comes alive with pastels as the first trees leaf out. A rush of darker greens follows, each species racing to get ahead of the others in an apparent frenzy to color the hillsides. Shortly, the leaves will close us in, making us feel as if we are now wrapped in a green cocoon. The world becomes quieter as some of our harsher human sounds are softened by the abundant foliage. The hills and valleys will soon be smothered in green, and the once open views will be gone until the leaves drop again next fall.

One spring I got to wondering just how many different shades of green there were. On my morning walks, I counted at least ten, but I was at a loss to describe them because the English language, normally so rich in descriptive words, lacks a vocabulary for such subtly different colors. Considering that we are surrounded by green for half the year, you'd think precise descriptive words might have evolved. I've read that the Eskimos, who are surrounded by snow and ice, have at least fifteen words to describe different kinds, and when I was in Mexico I learned that the Mexicans have ten terms for different kinds of blankets. Somehow we temperate North Americans seem to have neglected to develop a special vocabulary for our greens. So the best I can do is try to find the right adjectives—or combinations of adjectives—to describe the subtly different colors I see every spring.

As I walk along Schillhammer Road, I first have to acknowledge the greens that have been there all along—the deep evergreen-greens of pine and hemlock needles that are so much darker than the leaves just starting to unfold. The new young leaves of aspens, which are the first of the deciduous leaves to appear, start out pale—so pale they're almost yellow. They'll darken as they mature and chlorophyll builds in the leaf tissues, but they start out at the other end of the spectrum from the evergreens.

Soon the leaves of maples open, which are a darker green than the aspens, but their young leaves are often tinged with red and orange as if they're impatient to display the colors that should wait until fall. Then come the shiny greens of birch leaves and the lustrous green of beeches. Among the late leafers are the ashes and sumacs that grow along the roadside and fencerows. Their compound leaves add some new shades to the evolving mix. Feathery ash leaves appear a light and delicate green against the deep blue sky, and young sumac leaves display a bronze sheen in bright contrast to the other greens around them.

In the meantime, the ferns growing beneath my roadside trees have almost completely unfurled. One of them—the *interrupted fern*—offers two more colors. The yellow-green of their fronds is conspicuously "interrupted" by the dark blue-green of fertile leaflets near the middle of the plant. And new meadow grasses have grown up over the dead brown clumps left from last year, covering the barren ground with what looks like a bright green carpet.

This wonderful assortment of greens will soon disappear. As summer progresses, all these greens will darken with the buildup of chlorophyll—the great equalizer. The landscape will become more uniformly deep green. Although there are still slight differences here and there, I can hardly detect them as I walk along my road.

When all these new leaves emerge at the beginning of the growing season, they're fresh, young, and perfect, like newborn babies. But as the season progresses they're soon found by animals and insects, and by midsummer most of them are covered with warts, bumps, and holes. Perhaps this is the way of life: one is born perfect, but over time the signs of living give a worn look. Deciduous trees, however, have something going for them. They can drop their old leaves every fall and start again with new ones come spring.

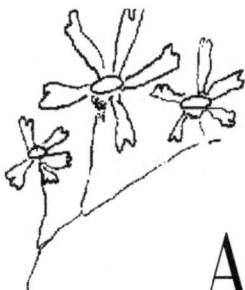

Arrival of Summer

Sometime in late May or early June I sense that the landscape has given itself over entirely to green. The forested hillsides are now green clear to the top, and when I poke into my woods I feel as if the trees around me have finally arrived at the moment they've been preparing for all year. Their new leaves are almost fully formed, and the once limp branchlets are now stretching out and reaching up to present these new leaves to the sun.

As tree leaves mature, they arrange themselves in a pattern that enables them to capture the maximum amount of sunlight. At first they're all in competition with their neighbors, but eventually they compromise so that, working together, they'll be able to absorb as much energy as possible for the tree to use.

Small trees and saplings along the forest edge are already showing significant growth. They've formed thickets that appear impenetrable. Only a month ago, I could look into the leafless woods and see a deer a quarter of a mile away, but now the foliage is so dense it would hide a whole herd of deer just the other side of a thicket.

Soon the new twigs and leaves will reach their maximum size and growth will stop for the rest of the summer. Curious to see how much growth had occurred so far, I measured some of the sprouts on sugar maples and ashes in my woods and found that they were almost two feet long. Less than a month ago, these twigs didn't exist, which means they grew almost an inch a day! It's amazing to think that everything needed to produce this year's twigs and leaves could have been tightly packed inside half-inch buds, and that such prodigious growth could occur in so short a time.

Trees do this by making all the necessary cells for new growth during the previous summer and packing them into the buds. When spring's snowmelt and rains offer water, these cells begin to expand, forcing the buds to break. The cells then continue to expand, filling with water much as a balloon fills with air, until all the new leaves and branches gain their full size.

My maples, ashes, and basswoods show the most impressive growth, while the pines and hemlocks are much slower to put forth their new shoots. Only now, late May and early June, are the "candles" at the tips of pine branches beginning to expand and the small bright green clusters of new needles beginning to speckle dark hemlock crowns.

The colorful woodland wildflowers with their white, pink, red, and bluish colors are now gone from the forest floor. They've been replaced by the first roadside and field flowers of early summer, many of which—such as dandelions, mustards, and golden alexanders—are yellow. The yellows appear to be all the same shade, with none of the tonal variation I saw in the greens of early spring. I suspect that xanthophyll, which creates the yellow color, doesn't have the right chemistry to fashion so many variations.

Tent caterpillars are now enjoying a great feast as they chew on the new leaves of cherry and apple trees, creating messy tent-webs and denuding branches as they go. Their tents disfigure the roadside, but I appreciate the incredibly complex life cycle they undergo to survive. Through some evolutionary process, they have become nutritionally bonded to a specific group of plants in the rose family, namely cherries and apples, and they must feed on them exclusively. Their seasonal timing is therefore completely synchronized with the seasonal timing of these trees.

Now that summer is almost here, new sounds are in the air. Where winds once caused leafless branches to scrape and rattle, I now hear the pleasant rustling of leaves. And among these soft woodland sounds, I also hear the melodious songs of the ovenbird, veery, and wood thrush.

The changes that indicate the transition from spring to summer are different for different people, and summer certainly doesn't wait until June 21. Calendar dates have no real relationship to the forces of nature. My own indicator for the crossover is when dandelions stop blooming and buttercups begin—usually the first week in June in northern Vermont.

Summer is already the beginning of *next* year for trees. New buds are forming, filled with the cells that will become next year's twigs and leaves. After this year's leaves drop off, the buds will wait patiently for winter to pass. When the spring rains arrive, the buds will open, and the twigs and leaves will be ready to stretch out, reach up, and produce another burst of green.

Buttercups

When the dandelions have gone to seed and buttercups are in full bloom, I know summer is here.

The shiny yellow buttercup is often the first wildflower a child learns to recognize. I can remember grown-ups pressing one against my face and telling me they were buttering my cheek. A friend says her grandmother would hold one under her chin to see if she liked butter. Among other pleasant childhood memories is that buttercups meant school would soon be out for summer vacation.

By the third week of June here in Vermont, buttercups are at their peak. Their slender stems reach above the tips of dark green meadow grasses displaying bright yellow flowers that, from a distance, look like small flames suspended in air. Up close the plants are scraggly, with a cluster of deeply dissected leaves at the base and a long, largely bare stem. An early botanist thought buttercup leaves looked like crows' feet and named the family it belongs to the "crowfoot family." With leaves that look like birds' feet and long scraggly stems, buttercups make their best appearance when mixed with grasses or other plants that mask their ungainly appearance.

Buttercups prefer moist soils and thrive in wet meadows. The leaves and stems contain a bitter juice that grazing animals have learned to avoid. Their scientific name, *Ranunculus acris,* refers to this feature, *acris* meaning acrid or bitter. As the cows and horses graze around these unappetizing wildflowers, they remove the competing plants, giving buttercups room to flourish.

Insects, including my honey bees, don't seem to like buttercups either, but these resourceful flowers have developed a pollination strategy that doesn't depend on them. If you look down on a buttercup from above, you'll see that the five petals are arranged to form a bowl or cup. The inside of the cup looks shiny as if it's been waxed, but if you look down toward the bottom of the cup, you'll see that the bases of the petals are dull and soft.

This difference in petal texture aids in pollination. A water droplet sticks to the lower part of the petals but extends upward to where the petals are waxy. Pollen collects on the upper part of the droplet and is slowly lowered onto the stigmas, or pollen receptors, as the water drains from the bottom of the cup. This design assures reproduction without the help of insects, but in the past insects may have played a role. If you pull one of the petals out of the flower, you will see a tiny gland at its base that may once have produced nectar to attract them.

Buttercups boast an ancient heritage and were around long before such plants as dandelions and daisies. Indeed, their beginnings can be traced back 150 million years to when dinosaurs roamed the earth and the first flowering plants were just beginning to evolve. They are related to other primitive groups such as magnolias and laurels. One cannot help but respect a small plant that has had the tenacity to survive over such a long period of time.

Buttercups are not native to North America, but they arrived with the early European settlers and followed them across the country. They are now so abundant that it's hard to imagine they were not always part of our landscape. Buttercups thrive in cold, wet climates, which is why they are so abundant in Vermont. We are fortunate to have such a bright and familiar wildflower coloring our roadsides and meadows to help us enjoy summer.

Dandelions

As summer arrives, I notice the fuzzy gray seed heads of dandelions everywhere I look. These ghostly globes appear along roadsides, in meadows, and on lawns, each golf-ball-sized head at the top of a thin stalk stretched to its limit. The fuzzy gray "hairs" on the head soon serve as parachutes to carry the dandelion's seeds away on passing breezes.

Some of these fuzzy globes form perfect spheres. Those are the ones with all their seeds still attached to the small white cap at the tip of the stalk. Others that have lost some of their seeds appear lopsided and disheveled. Still others are bare with only the white cap remaining to show the base that anchored the seeds before they flew. A close look at the cap will reveal tiny scars where the seeds were attached, and if you look even more closely you'll see that these scars are arranged in a perfect spiral.

Indeed, a plain old dandelion is surprising in many ways, not only in its beautiful symmetry but also in its reproductive strategies.

The fuzzy dandelion head is made up of many dozens of seeds, each produced by an individual flower. What we think of as the dandelion's flower is really a cluster of flowers, each capable of being pollinated and producing its own seed. These small densely packed blooms look like petals radiating from the center of the head, but each of these "petals" has a male part that produces pollen and a female part that can receive pollen and produce a seed. Dandelions have three strategies for producing their seeds, and they are very protective of their flowers until the seeds are fully formed and ready to be dispersed.

While the young flowers are developing, they're tightly enclosed in slender green modified leaves, called *bracts,* that protect them from birds and insects. When the flowers are mature, the bracts open to expose them so they can be pollinated, but each night they close protectively again until morning when they reopen to give the flowers another shot at pollination. When the dandelion is ready to form its seeds, the bracts close tightly to protect the seeds until they're mature. Then they reopen one last time to enable the seeds to fly away.

Each small dandelion flower is programmed to make sure a new offspring will arise from it one way or another. First it strives for cross-pollination. The anthers—or pollen producers—form a cylinder through which the stigmas—or pollen receptors—must grow. But the stigmas remain pressed tightly together as they pass through the anthers until they're high enough above them that they can't be self-pollinated. Only then do they unfold and wait for pollen from another flower to come along.

After a time, however, the stigmas begin to curl downward until they eventually make contact with their own anthers. If they haven't been cross-pollinated, they can at this point be self-pollinated, which is better than nothing. But the dandelion has yet a third strategy, because even if pollination has taken place, it may not lead to a fertilized egg and embryo. Often, as the flower matures and goes through its pollination processes, some of the cells from the female part will grow into an embryo that will become incorporated into the seed. If pollination has failed, the seed with this self-produced embryo will grow into a genetically identical plant. This ultimate backup strategy explains why the jagged edges of the dandelion leaves in some populations look exactly alike—it's because they're clones.

The dandelion's fail-safe reproductive strategies make me appreciate the natural world and all the evolutionary forces that have made it as it is today. They also make me appreciate plain old dandelions that are so amazingly well-adapted for survival, whatever their circumstances. When I see them going to seed at the end of their annual cycle, I can't resist blowing on their heads to help the parachutes fly away.

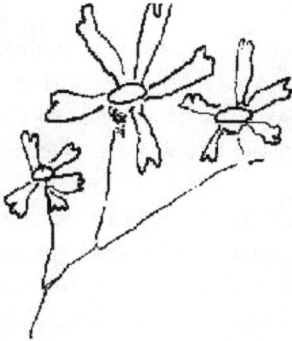

Fireflies

I t's a warm evening in early July, and my meadow is alive with flashing lights.

Hundreds of fireflies cruise low over the grasses, blinking repeatedly as they go. These are the males blinking in hopes of being noticed by a receptive female hidden in the grass below. Of all the strategies various organisms use to engage with the opposite sex, nothing compares to the unique, light-based courtship of the firefly.

The male's abdomen glows and glows again, the pattern of pulsating flashes sending silent signals to potential mates. The females perch on stalks of grass, watching for the right pattern of flashes. When a female sees the signal she's waiting for, she responds with flashes of her own that invite the male to come closer. The two flash back and forth several times as the male approaches, and when he arrives they mate.

Afterwards the female quits flashing, while the male returns to his cruising altitude and resumes his light show in hopes of attracting the attention of another available mate. Researchers have learned that in the firefly species most common in my area of Vermont, *Photinus pyralis*, males far outnumber females, and each male has only about ten chances to mate. He can't afford to waste time between matings.

As if having to compete with so many males of his own species isn't enough, Photinus pyralis males also risk being eaten by a predatory female belonging to another species. This species has learned to imitate the flashes of other fireflies and lure unsuspecting males to their death. The female gains an extra meal to sustain her and improve her own prospects of mating and laying eggs, and by eating the male she ingests a poisonous chemical he has in his system that offers added protection from spiders and birds. After she's eaten, she returns to flashing her own species' signal to attract a male she actually wants to mate with.

After mating, female fireflies lay their eggs in soil. A few weeks later, the eggs hatch into hungry larvae that spend the rest of the summer feeding on earthworms, snails, slugs, and other creatures they find in the dirt. Small as they are (only a few millimeters long), they can bite their victim and inject it with a fluid that will both paralyze and liquefy it to make it edible. To protect themselves from would-be predators, firefly larvae produce a glow of their own to warn that they are poisonous.

When the weather turns cold in fall, the larvae burrow into the soil for the winter. Next spring, they will pupate and metamorphose into adult fireflies ready to mate. At this point the adults can turn their lights on and off at will, which is highly unusual among bioluminescent creatures. Firefly light comes from an interaction of four substances: luciferin, adenosine triphosphate (ATP), luciferase, and oxygen. It's the luciferin that glows, but only if luciferase is added to it, plus ATP, in the presence of oxygen. The resulting light is considered cold light, with very little energy lost to heat. For comparison, a regular incandescent light bulb loses 97 percent of its energy to heat, while the firefly loses ten percent or less.

More than 2,000 species of firefly exist worldwide, over one hundred seventy of which live in the United States, mostly east of the Rocky Mountains. While each species has its own unique series of flashes for mating, and most mate individually, some Asian species have become famous for congregating and synchronizing their flashes. Thousands of those males collect in trees along river banks and all flash at the same time, creating quite a spectacle.

Until the early 1990s, scientists thought that only Asian species synchronized their flashes, but a woman who grew up in Tennessee reported that her family observed synchronous flashing every summer around their mountain cabin near Elkmont. Researchers arrived and confirmed that these Tennessee fireflies were indeed synchronizing their flashes. Once word was out, additional reports came in from Texas, North Carolina, Georgia, and South Carolina.

I wish all the fireflies I see flying above my meadow on warm July nights would suddenly decide to gather in one of my big sugar maples and impress the whole neighborhood with a grand spectacle of synchronized flashing.

I don't think it's going to happen, but imagining it takes me back to my childhood fascination with fireflies. I would go out into our suburban-Buffalo yard on a summer night and watch their flashes closely. Then I would chase them, calculating where they would be between each flash. I'd catch as many as I could and hold them in a glass jar, and when I'd caught quite a few I'd shake the jar to make them emit more light. Sometimes the glow was almost bright enough to guide me home.

Now, many years later on my farm in Vermont, I wander outdoors at dusk to watch the meadow behind my house light up with fireflies. After an hour or two, their tiny lights diminish in number until they disappear altogether, forcing me to wait until the next night to continue my observations and fantasies.

Fungi Feasts

A s summer advances, the green vegetation that was so fresh and alive when it first appeared takes on a subdued look. About then I start to notice fungi that thrive in the heat and humidity of late summer. Until now they've remained hidden in the soil or deep in rotting wood awaiting the rains that will give rise to their fruiting bodies. The fungi's fruiting bodies are the familiar mushrooms we see on lawns, in the woods, along roadsides, and growing like shelves on tree trunks.

There's a part of the fungi we don't see, made up of thin threads called *hyphae*. The hyphae reach into and feed on decaying organic matter, growing into a dense tangle called a *mycelium*. When the time, temperature, and moisture are right, the mycelium produces fruiting bodies that mature and disperse spores to perpetuate the species.

The fresh young fruiting bodies of several species are edible for humans, and I have four favorites that appear around my house every year. The earliest is the *chanterelle*, which grows in my hemlock woods. Chanterelles look a bit like miniature yellow trees pushing up through the hemlock needles and spreading out their caps like little flat-topped elms. My son Tom finds them first and is good enough to share some of his harvest with me. He also finds a species of black chanterelle called the *trumpet of death*, which despite its name is edible. He dries enough of these favorites for both of us to eat at other times of year.

Another I especially like is the *puffball*—not the giant white puffball that can grow as big as a soccer ball, but a smaller brownish species that grows less visibly among my apple trees. These small puffballs look a bit like golf balls growing on short stalks. They have a soft, spongy feel when I cut them, and I always check to see that their inner flesh is pure white. The white flesh of the immatures is delicious, but when it begins to turn yellow the edible period is over. At that point, I wait patiently for my little puffballs to mature, and then I step on them, half for the fun of it and half to help them spread their dark spores.

My favorite end-of-summer mushroom is the *shaggy mane*, which is named for the shaggy appearance of its elongated cap. Shaggy manes are prolific, popping up in clumps along the road and on my lawn. Where I see one clump, if I look around a bit I'll often spot four or five more in the vicinity. If I pick some one day and go back the next, I'll find that more have grown overnight.

When I spot my first shaggy manes I inspect the individual mushrooms closely. Some of them are older than others, and I want the smallest, most intact mushrooms for eating. I try to eat them the same day I pick them, but if I can't I put them under water and eat them as soon as I can. In the meantime, the ones I didn't pick turn black, producing an inky fluid that can stain my clothes. At this stage they're often called inky caps, and they're not at all appetizing.

The last of my favorites, called *oyster mushrooms*, appear on the big maples in front of the house when the weather first turns cold. They show up every year, growing like overlapping shelves protruding from the parts of old trees that are dead or dying. Because the mushrooms grow at about eye level, I always rush to harvest them for fear someone else will notice them and get there before I do. Their flesh is firmer than other mushrooms and has a distinct oyster-like flavor.

I can't say I'm a gourmet chef when it comes to preparing and cooking mushrooms, but I know how I like them best. I wash them in the kitchen sink to get rid of the dirt, saute them in butter, sprinkle them with salt, and eat them while they're hot.

These late summer and fall mushrooms are the last wild edibles of the season. I feast on them as I find them, knowing that once they've gone by I'll have to wait until next year to enjoy them again.

Wooly Bears

In September the natural world around Schillhammer Road prepares for winter. Cooler and shorter days prompt both plants and animals to change in many ways. My maples are already showing bits of red and orange, and the chipmunks on the back porch are all at once stuffing their cheeks with sunflower seeds to cache for winter food.

It's a great time of year to observe what's happening in the biological world, and my morning walks always bring something new for me to think about. I saw woolly bear caterpillars crawling across Schillhammer Road one recent morning, and I stopped to look at them more closely than I have in the past. They were coming from the direction of the roadside hayfield, which I suspect is a favorite summer feeding ground. The cooler and shorter days of fall bring out large numbers of these fuzzy caterpillars, each one about two inches long with black at either end and a brown band in the middle. Their beady black eyes are hidden in the dense fur on their heads, so it's difficult to see which end is the front, but you can always tell by which direction they're moving.

Folklore has it that the width of the woolly bear's brown band is an indication of the kind of winter we're going to have: a wide band means a short, mild winter, and a narrow brown band means a long, cold winter. From what I've learned about woolly bears, the width of the band has less to do with the upcoming winter than it does with the past summer. The amount of brown is related to how old the caterpillar is, so if the summer has been long, with plenty of time for the caterpillar to feed and grow, there will be more brown. If summer came late or fall is arriving early, there'll be less brown. Some research has also correlated the width of brown bands with moisture—dry conditions produce wide bands, while wet conditions produce narrow bands.

I'm actually less interested in whether woolly bears can predict winter weather than I am in the direction and speed of their travels. On my one-mile walk I usually see at least ten woolly bears crawling along as if they know where they're going. I'm fascinated by the observation that most of them are headed in the same direction. One day I counted thirty woolly bears, twenty-one going south and nine going north. I noticed that those headed south were moving at a steady pace, while those going north moved more slowly and, to my mind, seemed confused. I gently turned a southbound woolly bear around and pointed it northward to see what it would do. It hesitated a few moments, then slowly turned itself back around to head south again. When I turned it around a second time, it sensed danger, curled into a tight ball, and played dead.

What causes their direction of travel isn't known, but I find myself wondering again if they're guided by polarized light from the sun, much as my honey bees use polarized light to guide them back to their hives.

Next I stretched a measuring tape beside a woolly bear heading south at a comfortable speed and determined that it was traveling two feet per minute. I measured two more and the pace was constant, which means they traveled about 120 feet an hour. If a woolly bear travels at that rate for ten hours of daylight, it can cover about 1,200 feet a day, which adds up to over a mile in five days. Not bad for such a small creature, but I calculate it would take a woolly bear six hundred days to travel from Schillhammer Road to the Massachusetts border, which means it's probably not trying to migrate toward a warmer climate. My southbound woolly bears are probably just looking for a more protected place than a hayfield to spend the winter. Whatever they're up to, migrating is part of their annual preparation for winter, and the best of them will appear again next spring. Nature has provided the genetic coding to make sure that the species will behave as they must to survive.

Watching woolly bears—and wondering about them—makes me mindful of how little we really know about the natural world. Scientists continue to discover new facts to explain some behaviors of some species, but there's still much to learn, including about the humble woolly bear. As a scientist myself I enjoy exploring new ideas, but in my heart I hope we will never learn all of nature's secrets. I'm content to watch my woolly bears crawling purposefully across Schillhammer Road and let the why's and where-to's remain a mystery.

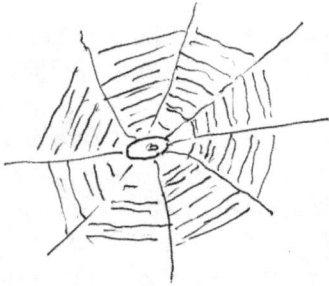

Spider Webs

Not long after I noticed the woolly bears moving south across Schillhammer Road, I began seeing fresh new spider webs in the hayfield the woolly bears were leaving. I've always been fascinated by how spiders spin their webs, especially orb webs like those in my hayfield.

To begin, the orb weaver perches on a high point—in this instance a tall stalk of grass—and releases a single strand of silk that is carried by the wind to another stalk of grass. This strand provides support for the rest of the entire web. After the strand is attached, the spider crawls along its length and establishes a network of radial strands like spokes in a bicycle wheel. Finally, the spider spins a carefully spaced spiral outward from the center, anchoring it to the spokes as it goes. The spider then crawls back in toward the center, adding sticky, insect-catching silk to the spiral. When it gets back to the center this time, it's ready to rest there and wait patiently for an insect to fly into the web.

The spider mating ritual is different for each species. In one case, the male spider plucks the strands of its web to get the attention of a female. Some spiders dance in front of the female. For the one I like best, the male presents a fly to the female before mating.

When I walked into the hayfield that day to look more closely at webs I'd spotted from the road, I made an amazing discovery. There had been three days of rain, and now, on this clear morning, I saw seven fresh, new orb webs suspended among the taller grasses, and all of them were facing in exactly the same direction that most of the woolly bears were traveling. I wondered once again whether some force, perhaps the polarized light that guides my honey bees, guides the spiders too. The question stayed with me as I observed the webs in my field.

Each delicate, perfectly formed web was about fifteen inches across, and each had a spider waiting at the center, waiting for a fly. I was reminded of the giant radio telescope dishes that point to distant galaxies. Do spiders know something we don't? Years ago, I attended a seminar where a NASA scientist reported on experiments with animals, including spiders, to see how they would respond to a weightless environment in space. The first web spun by one of the experimental spiders was a tangled mess, but its second was perfect. What had happened after that first web that enabled the spider to produce a perfect second? Another question to file away for answers another day.

After several days of pondering why all the spider webs would be facing in the same direction the woolly bears were traveling, it dawned on me that the two had nothing to do with each other. The spiders' webs were positioned not by polarized light or the seasonal impulse to travel to a safer place for winter but by the *wind*. Because in my neighborhood the prevailing winds are from the west, the spiders' first long strands of silk were blown from west to east, which oriented their webs north-south. And since settling on the south sides of their webs would provide the spiders with more warmth from the sun, it made sense that that's where they were.

Once again I have discovered that there are still plenty of things for me to learn about on Schillhammer Road. As the seasons continue to pass, I'm sure the biological world will continue to present me with the kinds of questions I've always enjoyed thinking about and finding the answers to. I am reminded of a quotation attributed to Thomas Edison that says, "We don't know one millionth of one percent about anything."

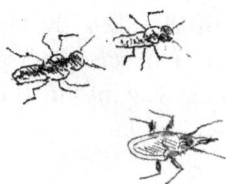

Bugs in the House

My farmhouse was built in 1810. The builders constructed its frame from large, hand-hewn timbers. Then they stood wide, white pine boards vertically to form walls and covered the outside with clapboards. It's a comfortable house for human beings to live in—cool in summer, warm in winter—and it was a pleasant home for generations of farm families before mine took up residence in 1958. But over the years I have learned that it's also comfortable for a host of other creatures.

Because the house is old, it has more than the usual number of cracks and holes for mice, chipmunks, and squirrels to crawl through—and they do. I try to plug the openings wherever I find them, but these determined rodents always find new ways to get in. In addition to the furry mammals, various insects also find their way inside. Many of them arrive at predictable times of year, and I can almost tell the season by which insect I see in my house.

The earliest to enter in the fall is the cricket that finds its way into my living room after the early frosts, usually in late September around here. Heralding the arrival of autumn, the cricket chirps loudly from behind the sofa or under my chair. How it gets in, I don't know, but one does every year. I chase the noisy bug around my living room as it leaps just ahead of my grasping hands. Eventually I catch it and toss it back outdoors where it belongs.

The next invaders are the cluster flies that gather on the clapboards on the sunny side of my house and then squeeze in around even the tightest of window frames. They look a bit like houseflies, but they're bigger, slower, and more bothersome. Once inside, they fly about, bumping into sunny windows and lamp shades. I never understand why these flies go to the trouble of squeezing their way into my house only to bang themselves against bright windows and lamps trying to get back out.

Cluster flies are tough to get rid of, but I found one way to control them, at least in my bathroom. I noticed that the gray spiders spinning webs under the eaves of the porch were capturing flies. I took one small, fuzzy spider and placed it on the bathroom ceiling above the night-light that attracted cluster flies. The spider, which I named Harry, immediately spun a web and began to catch and devour the flies. It gave me great pleasure and satisfaction to hear the frantic buzzing as they tried to escape from the web. Harry spent the winter doing away with dozens of cluster flies, and by spring he had grown to twice his original size. I took fat Harry back out and released him onto the porch ceiling where he could spin a new web and return to catching his own choice of flies.

Another fall intruder is a slow-moving wasp. It belongs to the species that builds usually small, papery gray nests that look like exposed honeycombs. Only a few find their way into my house about the same time that cluster flies show up. The wasps crawl sluggishly across the windowpanes—unlike the cluster flies, who bump and bumble—trying to find their way back out. They don't seem especially threatening, but they're capable of stinging, so I usually open the window for them anyway.

Around Halloween my house is invaded by ladybugs. Since they will feed on the aphids that bother my houseplants, I welcome them. I'm used to the ladybugs I see around my garden during the summer, but these late fall home invaders belong to a different species that was imported from Asia. They're so noticeable around Halloween that they have been nicknamed *Halloween beetles*.

My favorite insect is the assassin bug that shows up indoors during the winter. Where they come from I don't know, but one appears every year. It's a fierce looking bug with a black body and long snout it uses to stab other insects. It injects its prey with a powerful substance that liquefies the insides, and then the assassin bug sucks the liquefied tissues right out. I've read that an assassin bug can even shoot its poison some distance to obtain its dinner. I often place a resident assassin bug on my potted houseplants, where it's happy to eat aphids for a while, but then it somehow finds its way into the bathtub, where I catch it and place it on a new plant.

For nearly two hundred years, the human inhabitants of this old farmhouse have had to share their quarters with the many creatures who have needed a place to come in out of the cold. Like my predecessors, I'm learning to live with the various bugs who choose to make my house their cold-weather home.

Fall Colors

By the second week of October the trees in my neighborhood are ablaze with color. The leaves are yellow, orange, red, and many shades in between. It is the peak of Vermont's fall foliage season, every year attracting tourists from all over the world. Indeed, there is no other region in the world that has the right combination of tree species and weather to produce the brilliant colors Vermont can show off.

From my house in Schillhammer Road, I can see the trees on distant hills and tell the species of tree by their hue. The bright red of maples stands out most, followed by the yellow-orange of sugar maple. Birches and aspens, which were bright green all summer, are now golden yellow, while the beeches are turning from yellow toward a coppery brown. The red maples near my house have turned dark crimson, while the sugar maples that line my stone wall are still adding to their rich array of yellows, flaming oranges, and brilliant reds. When the sun shines through these fall leaves, the colors are intensified, and the trees seem to compete for my attention.

This spectacular display doesn't happen overnight. As the days shorten after the summer solstice, the shifting ratio of daylight to darkness eventually triggers changes in the tree's relationship to its leaves, but most of what happens is imperceptible until September, when the leaves begin to show a bit of color.

The cool temperatures of fall speed up these invisible processes, and the colors that begin to appear are the first visible indication that the leaves are dying. But before they die, the cells at the base of each leafstalk must go through some important changes. They form what's called an *abscission layer* that gradually cuts off the nutrient transport system to the leaf.

During the time this abscission layer is developing, chlorophyll— the great, green equalizer of summer—gradually breaks down and disappears. Colors that had been present in the leaves all summer but were masked by the dominant chlorophyll begin to show through. Pigments called *xanthophylls* turn some leaves shades of yellow, while *carotenoids* turn others yellow-orange. In some species, pigments called *anthocyanins* develop in sap that's trapped in the dying leaves, producing the flaming oranges and brilliant reds that make Vermont's fall foliage so spectacular. By the end of the season, the abscission layer has become so dry and corky that the leaves are forced to drop off, leaving behind preformed scar tissue to protect the tree through winter.

But this day is special. There was a gentle rain during the night and some of the leaves glisten with rain drops still clinging to them. This morning, I walked my dog along the road, admiring colors that weren't there two weeks ago. I paused a moment to savor the view and, looking up into the crown of a sugar maple, I saw a leaf drifting downward like a giant snowflake.

I watched its descent until it reached the road, joining thousands of others that had fallen earlier. This leaf had been born in spring and spent the summer photosynthesizing to make sugar. It had now finished its work and there was nothing more to do except return to the soil.

Looking up into the crown from which it came, I saw thousands more leaves that, like this one, spent the summer drawing water from the soil and taking carbon dioxide from the air, and—using energy from the sun—made sugar to nourish the tree on which they grew. The leaves in a tree crown form a giant photosynthetic factory, wonderfully organized to capture the sun's energy. When their work is done, like my lone maple leaf, each separates from the tree and falls to the ground.

Looking more closely at my leaf, I observed its functional structure, designed to maximize exposure to the sun. Its stalk holds the blade— the larger part of the leaf—at the best angle to capture sunlight. The venation, or ribbing, holds the leaf firmly, preventing it from collapsing. Besides offering support, each vein must transport water and sugar to and from the leaf. The orientation of thousands of leaves in a tree to capture maximum sunlight is an incredibly synchronized feat.

Even the shape of the leaf has a function, and every tree has its own signature. One can only wonder at the role the lobes of a maple leaf or the toothed margin of a beach play in the life of the trees. In the course of evolution, a close relationship always exists between form and function. The sharp points at the tip of the lobes of a maple leaf, for instance, are thought to bleed storm water from the leaf's surface to help prevent fungal growth.

Holding the leaf in my hand, I continued my walk, thinking about this relationship between form and function in living organisms. I came upon a butternut tree with branches overhanging the road, dropping butternuts like small cannon balls. I dodged one and, looking into the crown, saw a squirrel cutting them from the branches. At the end of the day, I counted fifty-one nuts. The next morning, they were all gone.

The end of summer and the arrival of fall is a bittersweet time of year with its bright autumn colors and clear blue skies. Ahead are frosty days and the beginning of winter. In the meantime, I will make the most of enjoying colors in the landscape that I won't see again for another year.

With that thought, I dropped the leaf onto the road so it could return to the earth.

November

As October gives way to November, I see major changes happening. A quiet, almost serene quality has settled over the woodlands and meadows. The birds that were everywhere only a few weeks ago have mostly disappeared. There are no more honking geese, and I miss the thrill of seeing their precise V's against the autumn sky. Just as when I was a boy, I still feel a tug inside my body when they fly overhead, but they're gone for the season now.

I find myself wondering if all my life I've been responding in some ancient and primitive way to the same forces that call the birds to flee winter. As I listen to the birds that are still around, I hear an occasional crow and sometimes the raucous call of a raven, but there are no robins or other song birds. I think I miss most the melodious song of the wood thrush that so characterizes the rich sounds of a Vermont summer. Even the chipmunks and squirrels that hang around under my bird feeders are now scarce.

But along with my yearning to flee, too, I also see reasons to stay. The leafless trees mean that once again I can see far into the woods. A thick blanket of fallen leaves covers the forest floor, hiding all except the mossy, lichen-covered boulders and evergreen ferns. I can now see clumps of Christmas fern that were obscured by the greenery of summer, and I notice how many of them there are scattered throughout the woods. Their dark green fronds look elegant and invite me to look more closely. They thrive in the cool, moist air as do the mosses and lichens, which seem rejuvenated under the darkening skies and shorter days.

173

The countryside around my house has taken on a soft quality and feels like it's going to sleep. As the days grow shorter, the light dims and is noticeably weak even at the peak of the day. But under the right conditions, this subdued light is warm.

As the sun sinks lower in the sky, its filtered rays cast a reddish tone over the landscape, and some of Vermont's most glorious sunsets occur at this time of year. Some late afternoons, a peach-shaded glow suffuses the wooded hillsides, creating colors that weren't there during summer. New tones of yellows and browns appear among the meadow grasses, and the edges of blades that have been touched by frost have turned a pinkish red. Looking out over the meadow I notice that the texture of the hummocks and tussocks has changed as the longer shadows give a depth that was not there before.

Leafless trees reveal their trunks and limbs against the November sky, showing shapes and forms that were hidden during summer. The sugar maples display their strong, upward-reaching, angular branches, while the ashes stand rigid, holding their stiff branches outward. As sunlight strikes the leafless trees, it highlights the color of their bark. The blacks and grays make strong signatures against the soft mauve background.

As the days grow shorter, all the forces of nature are at work to prepare for the coming of winter. I have always marveled at how many different ways living things respond to change. There's dormancy, migration, hibernation, and food storage, but there are other responses, too. These shorter fall days stimulate my local trout to breed, and snowshoe hares and weasels begin to change their fur color from brown to white.

Even humans change. Some take on new personalities, often tending toward depression as the light wanes. I used to watch my students become glum as the fall semester wore on, and I guess it wasn't always because of the school work. I think they too were responding to the shorter length of the day. I also suspected that the human immune system is weakened by shorter days because coughs and sniffles began to show up in the classroom as the season progressed, but I haven't tried to confirm this.

November is the winding down of autumn and the beginning of winter. Next year's tree leaves and flower buds are already in place, prepared to wait until days lengthen again next spring before springing back into action. Fat woodchucks have disappeared into their burrows to hibernate, and squirrels and chipmunks have enough seeds and nuts stored to feed them through the winter. I find myself hoping that I will make it through as well.

November is a month of ups and downs, and there are more downs than ups for those of us who worship the warm sun and long days of summer. I sometimes find myself envying those creatures whose genes tell them to hibernate comfortably over the winter—or maybe since I'm a botanist, I should envy the dormant plants that can rest all winter and start over again with new leaves and flowers in the warm sunshine of spring.

On Ice

When winter comes to Vermont, most folks wait for snow. I wait for ice.

As a longtime ice fisherman, I all but worship the time when the lake waters are frozen and ice has transformed the landscape into a new world of beautiful bleakness—a silent, uncluttered place that is a satisfying escape from all the noise and commotion of our modern society.

I enjoy the company of people, but when I fish I want to be alone. Walking on the ice to the farthest point from other fishermen is my goal. Once there I cut a hole and drop my line. Then, standing with my back to the wind, I can fish for hours in wonderful silence. I imagine it's like being on the moon. Life is timeless and hours pass as minutes. When I return home I feel refreshed and all is well with the world.

As the days shorten and temperatures drop, the water in lakes and ponds cools and the fascinating transformation to ice begins. Water is a remarkable liquid with a peculiar property: as it cools it becomes heavy and sinks to the bottom of a lake. But just before it's cold enough to freeze, it suddenly expands, rises to the surface, and then solidifies. An ice layer forms on the surface and freezes downward, rather than from the bottom up. If it were not this way our lakes and ponds in northerly latitudes would remain frozen solid year around. There's only enough heat from the summer's sun to melt the surface—much like permafrost in the Arctic—and we would not have life as we know it today.

Ice is almost magical. One day a lake surface is riffled with wave action. Then comes a frosty night with no wind, and the next day the surface is a shiny mirror of ice. If there's no snow, the ice is clear and you can walk on the water and look down to the bottom to see rocks, plants, and fish. It's an eerie sight. The first time I walked on clear ice and peered down at the lake bottom twenty feet below, my knees buckled, just as they do when I look straight down from a ten-story building.

But there are few days when totally clear ice forms, for when temperatures drop it usually means a storm front is approaching, and with a winter storm comes snow. The freeze and snow usually arrive together and you get milky ice with a rough, crusty snow cover. Even this cold, sculptured landscape has a charm of its own, though. As the wind blows the snow, it's swept into wave-like riffles and ridges, and the surface of a pond or lake looks like a desert.

Lake ice takes on all sorts of appearances, and each freeze is different from the last. Sometimes a lake is coated with a thin frozen layer no more than a half-inch thick. If it doesn't freeze deeper, strong winds can break it up only to refreeze it into a formidable mass of jagged pieces that look like thousands of broken window panes, their sharp edges pointing in all directions.

Ice is remarkably strong, too, and can withstand great weight when freshly frozen. Two inches will support a man, even a fat one. Seven inches will hold a car; eighteen inches will take a freight train. But newly formed ice is somewhat springy and will bend slightly under weight without breaking. A car driven over a typical frozen surface sends out ice waves that produce strange gulping noises. As the ice thickens and expands, it delivers an assortment of sounds that range from mere creaks and grinds to sharp cracks like a rifle shot, or great booms from a giant cannon. Subzero temperatures produce the loudest cracks and booms.

Sometimes the expansion is so great that pressures force the ice to fold up into huge ridges and broken slabs that can extend for a mile or more. These pressure ridges can rise five or more feet high, and often there's unfrozen water lying between the tilted blocks.

As winter progresses, the ice freeze reaches deeper and deeper below the surface, especially when there is no snow cover to insulate it. Sometimes ice can reach depths of three feet in Lake Champlain, and it's a chore to cut a hole to fish through. As the ice thickens, the expansive pressures are enormous, so huge blocks of ice are thrust up at the shoreline.

Finally the time comes when the ice must go. With the approach of spring, the sun's rays become more and more intense, burrowing into the ice, creating a honeycomb structure of narrow vertical columns as it melts. Later these columns will collapse, the ice becomes granular, and walking on it feels like you're on a surface of dry split peas.

For me, one of the most memorable moments in the demise of lake ice comes as rising waters lap at the edge of an eroding ice cover. As pencil-thin columns of ice fall away, they bump gently against each other and make a delicate tinkling sound like wind chimes. It's a fitting musical finale to the ice story, and I eagerly await another winter for the cycle to begin again.

Hub's mother, Martha Vogelmann, with Hub's grandson—
Martha Vogelmann's great grandson—Scott, under a red
maple in front of the Schilhammer Farm. The reddest tree
for miles around (Fall, 1980).

Hub and Marie's boys, Jim, Tom, and Andy,
on the family farm on Schillhammer Road.

Making repairs to the old CRS Wilhelm Farm,
aka Schillhammer Farm, which was Martha's place.
This barn eventually burned.

Son Tom Vogelmann and his children clear brush on the Schillhammer Farm (1991).

Grandkids playing on "the alligator," in the pond that shouldn't be there on Schillhammer Road.

Grandkids Connie, Alice, and Scott play in the gardens behind the farmhouse (1990).

Grandkids, Alice, Scott, and Connie (1993).

Granddaughter Alice holds a bouquet of dandelions behind the family farmhouse (1988).

Fixing the slate roof on Hub's greenhouse (1995).

Hub's sons speak no evil, hear no evil, see no evil: Jim, Tom, and Andy (2008).

Sons Andy and Tom in front of the fieldstone fireplace inside the family farmhouse (2008).

Tom's wife, Mary Neighbours, carries wood into the farmhouse (2011).

Hub on his John Deere tractor (2009).

Daugher-in-law Ann and son Jim before the
fieldstone fireplace at the farm on Schillhammer Road
(2009).

Hub stands beside the great boulder in the field on his farm
(2010).

Hub working with his bees (1995).

Hub and Mary Jane Dickerson (2002).

NASA Helicopter collecting data on Camels Hump
(1982). Special Collections, UVM Bailey-Howe Library.

Tom Siccama (1967).
Special Collections, UVM
Bailey-Howe Library.

Hub Vogelmann on
Camels Hump (1982).
Special Collections, UVM Bailey-
Howe Library.

NASA assisted research being conducted on Mount
Mansfield (c.1983-4). Special Collections, UVM Bailey-
Howe Library.

Fog Moisture Collector on Mount Mansfield.
Photo by T. Sherbatskoy, for Country Journal, 1983. Special
Collections, UVM Bailey-Howe Library.

Camels Hump in the 1960s. Special Collections, UVM
Bailey-Howe Library.

Camels Hump after 1982. Special Collections, UVM
Bailey-Howe Library.

IV.
Camels Hump
and Acid Rain

Fog collector

Friends who read early drafts of the materials I planned to include in this book offered suggestions about what I should change or add. One suggestion I found difficult to ignore was that I ought to say something about Camels Hump and acid rain. I had avoided these subjects because I didn't want to revisit all the politics and stress that evolved after I went public with what my own, my students', and my colleagues' research told us about the effects of acid rain on our much-studied mountain.

Even after I retired, I was invited to speak to community groups on the subject of acid rain, so Gale Lawrence, who was helping me organize my papers, created a thick notebook to take with me. It was full of all the clippings I had collected during those most intense and stressful years, plus several more she found by searching through old magazines and journals. I have donated this notebook to the University of Vermont's Special Collections along with all the photographs and slides I took at the time. Because these materials explain—and show—the whole acid rain story in more detail than I ever could, I figured they should let me off the hook. But I recognized that this book would be incomplete if I said nothing about what had occupied so much of my professional life.

So I decided to write a review of the research my students and I started doing back in the mid-1960s and that new generations of students and professors are still doing to this day. Because that review includes over forty years of work, I've divided it into two parts—Camels Hump Before 1982 and Camels Hump After 1982. I chose 1982 as the midpoint. That's the year I wrote "Catastrophe on Camels Hump," the article that changed my life and my relationship to the work we were doing. I've inserted the text of the article, which appeared in the November 1982 issue of *Natural History* magazine, because it summarizes a lot of important information. I've also included some retrospective thoughts on acid rain. And I end with an update, because more than twenty-five years after "Catastrophe on Camels Hump" acid rain is still in the news.

I hope that these final materials, combined with the photographs, slides, and thick notebook of clippings available at Special Collections, will satisfy those who want to know more about the work on Camels Hump and acid rain.   —   H. V.

Camels Hump
Before 1982

Viewed from the Champlain Valley, Camels Hump presents a distinctive profile. Early English settlers named it "Camels Rump," perhaps because they thought the mountain resembled that portion of a camel's anatomy, but the name was changed to Camels Hump in the 1800s. Earlier French explorers were a bit more romantic, calling it *le lion couchant* because they thought it resembled a reclining lion. Whichever name is most descriptive of the mountain's profile, Camels Hump is the one that stuck.

Located about fifteen miles south of Mount Mansfield, Camels Hump is one of the tallest peaks in the Green Mountains. Many early Vermonters thought it was indeed the tallest because it stood so prominently on the horizon with no other nearby peaks to diminish its apparent size. Legend has it that the question of whether Mount Mansfield or Camels Hump was taller was settled by a musket ball. A marksman stood at the highest point on Mount Mansfield and loaded his musket. As he lowered his sight to the top of Camels Hump, the ball rolled out, settling the issue for everyone who was there. Today, at a measured elevation of 4,393 feet, Mount Mansfield is unquestionably the tallest mountain in Vermont.

And Camels Hump is not even second-tallest, a distinction that goes to Killington Peak, which is 4,235 feet. According to the most recent maps, Camels Hump and Mount Ellen tie for third place at 4,083 feet, with two other mountains that are part of the long ridgeline south of Camels Hump deserving mention: Cutts Peak at 4,022 feet and Mount Abraham at 4,006 feet. Of all these high mountains, Camels Hump is the most recognizable both because of its profile and its solitary position on the skyline. When the first snowfall coats its summit, I find the lone mountain strikingly beautiful—almost majestic.

Unlike Mount Mansfield, Killington, Mount Ellen, and others of Vermont's mountains, Camels Hump's slopes have escaped the scars of ski trails, lift corridors, access roads, and resort construction. It stands pristine, with a wild quality that's been lost on the mountains sacrificed to the ski industry and vacation home development. Several hiking trails lead to the summit, but they are modest intrusions in an otherwise unspoiled environment. They serve only those with the energy and desire to climb the mountain, who are the ones who most appreciate it just as it is.

The lower slopes of Camels Hump support a mix of temperate forest trees dominated by sugar maple, beech, and yellow birch. More than eighty different species of trees, shrubs, and herbs grow here. During May, colorful flowers such as spring beauty, dogtooth violet, red trillium, and a host of others hurry to flower before the trees leaf out and close the canopy overhead. In only a few short weeks, the forest floor becomes so shaded that these early spring flowers die down to wait for the arrival of another spring.

Higher on the mountain, beech gradually gives way, leaving sugar maple and yellow birch to dominate. With another short rise in elevation, the forest is taken over by red spruce, balsam fir, and white birch, resembling the boreal forest that grows farther north. The understory here is often a tangle of hobblebush and ferns, while the number of herbaceous species drops to fewer than twenty. Most striking among these is the painted trillium, which provides a welcome splash of color in an otherwise drab environment. I've often thought that the painted trillium would make a more appropriate state flower for the Green Mountain State than red clover, which isn't even a native.

On the windswept summit are scattered patches of arctic-alpine vegetation. Alpine bilberry forms a low shrubby heath growing among the rocks above tree line, and Bigelow's sedge dominates a sedge meadow on the summit itself. This arctic-alpine vegetation is remarkably similar to what I saw when I visited the Canadian Arctic north of Knob Lake many years ago. Standing in the middle of one of these patches and looking down, I can almost forget I'm on top of Camels Hump and think I'm back in the eastern Canadian Arctic.

The research on Camels Hump began in the mid-1960s. As a new plant ecologist coming to the mountains of Vermont from the flat country of Michigan, I was struck by the zonation of forest vegetation along the mountain slopes. The mountains I explored were high enough to have a deciduous forest of sugar maple and beech on the lower slopes and a boreal forest of spruce and fir on the upper slopes. I thought it would be interesting to determine how the climate and soils along the slopes changed with elevation to produce the different forest zones. It would be a basic ecological study that would have relevance to many of Vermont's mountains.

When my graduate student Tom Siccama finished his masters degree and wanted to work on a doctorate, I suggested my idea to him and he liked it. Because Camels Hump was undeveloped, we decided to do the study there. Together we built several instrument shelters in my workshop using louvered window shutters I bought from a local lumberyard. Tom hauled them up Camels Hump, and that was the beginning of a long-term study that has led to an unparalleled database that is still important today in understanding both the effects of acid rain and the changes in forest composition that are taking place as the climate warms.

In the life of a professor, a few students stand out above the others. Tom Siccama was just such a student. He showed up at the University not long after I did, and I liked him because he was bright, energetic, and enjoyed working outdoors in all kinds of weather. He was also a free spirit—sometimes even a bit challenging for me to supervise—but he was independent and, given an assignment, he would work tirelessly until it was done. He was also a stickler for accuracy and took great pride in doing whatever he did well.

Tom was my first doctoral student, and I remain impressed by his scientific mind. For his dissertation, he proposed to document the changes in vegetation with increasing elevation and correlate these changes with soils and climate by setting out plots every two hundred feet of elevation from 1,800 to 3,800 feet. His transect spanned Camels Hump's temperate and boreal life zones, and at each of his plots he set out rain gauges, thermometers, and other instruments to measure variables.

Tom was an exceptional field scientist: a good observer who enjoyed gathering data. In fact he sometimes collected too much of it. We still have notebooks full of numbers that no one has been able to digest. Tom's dissertation filled two volumes in which he amassed nearly three years worth of data on precipitation, air and soil temperatures, humidity, wind speed, and whatever else he could measure along his transect. It is a remarkable piece of research and was not easy to do.

First he had to backpack all his equipment up the mountain. Then he had to read his instruments and record the data every week, which meant climbing the mountain in all kinds of weather throughout the year. In winter the snow could be two or three feet deep with a temperature of thirty below zero. He had to climb three miles up a steep trail, and when the access road could not be plowed, which was most of the winter, he had to add another two miles to his hike. His whole project was both physically and mentally demanding, and there are not many people who would have had the stamina to finish the job. But the end product was worth the effort. Because of Tom's detailed field work others have been able to explore new research directions, perform new experiments, and make new discoveries.

Perhaps the most interesting of Tom's discoveries occurred during the summers of 1964 and 1965. These were drought years in the Northeast, and there was little rain even at the higher elevations. Tom noted that even though there was no water in his rain gauges, the soils on the upper slopes remained wet. In fact they were at field capacity, which means the soil is holding all the water that can be held after gravitational water is drained away. This seemed unlikely because in addition to the scant rainfall, trees transpire water and further deplete soil moisture. Where was all this water coming from?

Tom noticed that when he climbed the mountain in clouds and fog his clothes became wet, which led him to wonder if the clouds that frequently covered the mountain's higher elevations could be contributing water to the forest. We designed a simple experiment using a window screen that we mounted on a post and aimed at the incoming winds. A gutter at the base of the screen collected water and drained it into a bucket. After the first week, we were astounded at the amount of water we had collected—nearly a pailful even with no rain at all during the period. Later experiments demonstrated that the needles of the spruces and firs captured tiny water droplets just as our screen had. As the needles gathered what we referred to as fog moisture, the droplets coalesced and dripped from the needle tips onto the forest soil just as rain does.

It seemed amazing to us that no one had ever studied this phenomenon before. Our studies showed that an average of six inches of water could be collected each year by spruce and fir needles capturing moisture from fog, and at the highest reaches of the boreal forest zone, where the winds are strongest and the fog most common, it could be as much as thirty inches. All this water percolates into the soil, eventually contributing to stream flow and groundwater supplies at lower elevations. Our findings were eventually used when writing Vermont's Act 250 legislation, which prohibits construction above 2,500 feet without a special permit. Because we had determined that this elevation was the most common base of cloud and fog formation, the authors of Act 250 had a reliable, research-based figure to work with.

Our Camels Hump research progressed year by year and student by student. They have focused on the composition of the different forests and detailed the ground cover vegetation. They have counted mountain asters, blue-bead lilies, wood sorrels, and other wildflowers and have also investigated mosses, ferns, fungi, algae, bacteria, and even slime molds. Camels Hump is, in fact, Vermont's most-studied mountain and may well be the most-studied mountain in the Northeast, if not in the whole country. It is an ideal place for research projects because the more we learn about it, the more we realize how much more there is to know.

I remember a sign that hung on the wall where I used to work out on an exercise bike. It was the Thomas Edison quotation: "We don't know a millionth of one percent about anything." How true, and what a wonderful thought for researchers young and old.

As students gathered more and more information, the mountain became better known. Then came an unexpected discovery, the most important one of all. In the late 1970s, we saw that trees at the upper elevations—mostly red spruces—were dying. They developed sickly brown needles and thinning crowns, and then they died. In 1979 we decided we should resurvey the forest exactly as Tom Siccama had in 1965 to see how much change had taken place. We were shocked to find that we had lost about 50 percent of the spruces since 1965, and trees were still dying. It was the first study in the United States to document recent forest decline that was possibly a result of postindustrial air pollution, especially acid rain.

When the editor of *Natural History*, which is published by the American Museum of Natural History in New York City, urged me to write an article about the dying forests on Camels Hump, I was alarmed enough by what we were witnessing that I did. He entitled the article I produced for his November 1982 issue "Catastrophe on Camels Hump," and the national attention it attracted stirred major controversy about the effects of acid rain on the environment.

My article appeared at a critical time because Congress was already working on clean air legislation, and the American Museum of Natural History invited me to come down to New York City to hold a press conference. They felt that what was happening was too important to miss a chance to inform the public, even though this was only the second time in their history that they had ever called a press conference. So there I was, standing under a portrait of Teddy Roosevelt, facing a bank of microphones and a room crowded with members of the press. All the major television stations carried the story, and I was interviewed by reporters from all over the world. From that point on my life changed dramatically. There was no longer any peace—at least not as I had known it before acid rain hit the media.

"Catastrophe on Camels Hump" offers an overview of what we knew about the new and controversial phenomenon called acid rain as of 1982, so I've included it as my next chapter.

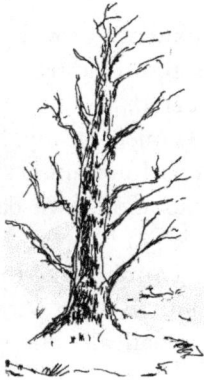

Catastrophe on Camels Hump

Twenty years ago the evergreen forests on the slopes of Camels Hump, a high peak in the northern Green Mountains of Vermont, were deep green and dense. The red spruces and balsam firs that dominated the vegetation near the mountaintop thrived under high rainfall and cool temperatures. The trees were luxuriant, the forest was fragrant, and a walk among the conifers gave one a feeling of serenity—a sense of entering a primeval forest. The upper slopes of Camels Hump have probably never been lumbered. Some red spruces more than three hundred years old reached one hundred feet into the sky, dwarfing the younger spruces and firs below.

Today the red spruces are dead or dying and some firs look sick. Gray skeletons of trees, their branches devoid of needles, are everywhere in the forest. Trees young and old are dead, and most of those still alive bear brown needles and have unhealthy looking crowns. Craggy tops of dead giant spruces are silhouetted against the sky. The brittle treetops often break off, leaving only a jagged lower trunk with a few scraggly branches. Strong mountain winds overthrow many dead trees, tipping upward their shallow root systems along with chunks of the forest floor. As more and more trees die and are blown down, the survivors have less protection from the wind, and even they are toppled over. The forest looks as if it has been struck by a hurricane.

As the tree canopy opens, the once shadowed forest interior is flooded with sunlight. An invasion of new vegetation is encouraged, but there are no young spruces to be seen. A luxuriant growth of ferns and shrubs now covers the once bare forest soil, providing a verdant carpet that belies the devastation that has occurred.

The dying of spruces is not restricted to Camels Hump. Spruces are succumbing throughout the northern Green Mountains, especially on the windward slopes at high elevations. Dead and crown-damaged trees are common in the Adirondack Mountains in New York, in the White Mountains in New Hampshire, in the Laurentian Mountains in Quebec, and in the Appalachians as far south as West Virginia. It is a disaster that, in a few short years, has dramatically changed the appearance of high mountains.

Elsewhere in the Northern Hemisphere similar events are occurring. Between two and a half and five million acres of forest in Central Europe are reported to have been damaged. In West Germany alone, thousands of acres of spruce and fir forests have died, and some scientists claim this is only the first signal of an environmental disaster. At the edge of the Alps in Bavaria, a state of West Germany, a reported 13,500 acres of conifers are doomed. Conifers are not the only trees in trouble; the natural regeneration of beech in the Ruhr Valley has almost ceased. Similar accounts of embattled forests are coming in from England, France, Switzerland, Yugoslavia, Czechoslovakia, and Poland. Die-back patterns of spruce like that occurring in Vermont have been noted in Sweden.

As the reports accumulate, scientists are stepping up their efforts to determine what is killing the forests. Camels Hump is a unique resource for evaluating possible causes of the devastation. It is a mountain that has been intensely studied since the mid-1960s, when Tom Siccama, then a graduate student at the University of Vermont, made a thorough study of the mountain's vegetation, climate, and soils. By counting and measuring trees, he established a detailed database that is of incalculable value today. Using the Siccama data for comparison, researchers at the University of Vermont have been able to document that nearly 50 percent of the spruces in the Camels Hump forest have died since 1965. Tree density, basal area (a measure of the amount of standing wood), and seedling reproduction also declined by 50 percent.

One possible explanation is that a disease or insects are destroying the red spruce, a species noted for being susceptible to such afflictions. In the late 1800s a beetle infestation caused widespread losses of spruces in the Adirondack Mountains and in New England. However, we have not found any insects on Camels Hump spruces that could cause the current mortality. Fungal growth is found under the bark at the bases of the dying trees, but plant pathologists believe these fungi are secondary invaders and only attack trees that are already dying.

Long-term population cycles must also be considered since large shifts in population numbers occur in many species over time. Fir trees, for example, sometimes grow in thick stands and mature as a group. A few years after they reach maturity, they die and the fir forest collapses. But the dying spruces do not fit this pattern: trees of different ages spread out over a wide area are dying all at the same time.

Another possibility is that the climate has changed recently and the effects on spruce are just now being realized. There was a period of dry years in the 1960s and again in the 1970s. Perhaps the effects of drought are now showing up in the spruces, which grow best in wet and cool climates. Periods of drought occur fairly regularly, however, and are a normal part of long-term weather cycles. Many of the dying trees are three hundred years old, and some are even older. It seems unlikely that there have been any changes in climate that these older trees have not confronted before.

With many of these normal causes of tree mortality ruled out, suspicions have turned to one ingredient of our environment that has been introduced in the last thirty years—acid rain. Could acid rain be responsible for the killing of our forests? That acid ran has damaged or destroyed fish life in hundreds of lakes in Europe and North America has been firmly established, but proving its impact on forests is extremely difficult because forests grow slowly and are subject to a wide variety of influences. Nevertheless, mounting evidence indicates that acidic rainfall may be impairing forest productivity and killing trees in several regions.

Acid rain is a modern-day product—a result of the industrial revolution and of all the tall smokestacks and car exhausts that are part of an affluent society. The burning of fossil fuels produces millions of tons of sulfur and nitrogen oxides. Spewed into the atmosphere, these gases combine with water and make sulfuric and nitric acids, which continually fall on the leaves of plants, enter the soil, and are added to lakes and streams. Just how acidic the rain has become can be determined by comparing it with the rain of preindustrial times. Frozen deep within the Greenland icecaps are annual layers of precipitation spanning thousands of years. Studies of samples of this frozen rain have revealed that the rain now falling in the northeastern United States is at least thirty to forty times more acidic than preindustrial rain.

Compounding the problem of acidity, smokestacks and car exhausts push other pollutants into the atmosphere—lead, zinc, copper, vanadium, and cadmium. These heavy metals are all toxic to plants, altering the permeability of cell membranes and interfering with the exchange of substances vital to the life of cells.

In the United States, acid rain is especially common in the Northeast, but the area it affects has enlarged dramatically since the 1950s and now stretches from the Mississippi River to the Atlantic coast; much of eastern Canada is affected too. Acid rain is now also common in California and the Rocky Mountains. It is well documented throughout Europe and has recently been reported from China.

Acid rain knows no political boundaries. Pushed by the wind, polluted air masses dump acid rain and heavy metals on whoever is downwind. What originates in the stacks of coal-burning plants in the Midwest falls on New England and eastern Canada. What is born in Canada gets exported to the eastern United States. In Europe, acid rains originating in England, France, and Germany eventually drop in Denmark, Norway, and Sweden. As the biological and economic impacts of acid rain become more clear, political clashes between countries will intensify.

While politicians fret about whose pollution is crossing whose borders, scientists from different parts of the world are gradually piecing together the puzzle of just how acid rain may harm the regions it falls on. New England, for example, is at the end of an enormous, heavily polluted airshed fed by prevailing westerly winds that carry pollutants for hundreds of miles. High mountains in the Northeast cause the air masses to rise and cool, forming precipitation in the form of rain, hail, snow, sleet, or drizzle—all acidic. To make matters worse, the affected area is also composed of young glacial soils, which are naturally acidic and devoid of the lime that could neutralize the sulfuric and nitric acids. Consequently, the acids combine with valuable nutrients, such as calcium, magnesium, sodium, and potassium, and leach them at an accelerated rate from already poor soils.

Some of the acid rain falls directly on the leaves of plants. There, too, it leaches away important substances needed for healthy growth, including potassium, sugars, proteins, and amino acids. Severe acid rains can even damage the waxy covering that protects leaves from desiccation and attacking fungi and bacteria.

Forests in the north country get an additional acid boost in the spring. Snow and ice, which accumulate for three or four months in winter, release acid in a sudden burst during the spring thaw, producing a strong shock to tree root systems as the acid percolates into the soil. Fogs that sweep through the forests on the mountaintops are often one hundred times more acidic than normal rain, more than twice as acidic as acid rain.

High elevation spruce-fir forests, such as the ones we've been studying on Camels Hump, receive much more rainfall and fog than do forests at lower elevations. Forests at 3,500 to 4,000 feet in the northern Green Mountains get about twice the annual precipitation of Burlington, Vermont, which is thirty miles away at an elevation of 400 feet. The acid load is more than doubled, and so is the dose of toxic heavy metals. Moreover, spruce-fir forests at high elevations are growing in a severe subarctic climate with a short growing season and on soils that are thin, nutritionally depauperate, and naturally acidic. These trees, already growing in a harsh environment, may be highly susceptible to the added insults of acid rain and heavy metals.

But are trees in marginal environments the only vulnerable plants? Perhaps the dying spruces are the equivalent of the canary in the mine, a warning of imminent danger to trees that are now growing in more favorable sites. Accumulation of heavy metals and steady acid rains may eventually tip the balance of life, a balance that may be more delicately poised than we realize.

This theory is now being tested in laboratory experiments and fieldwork at the University of Vermont. A team of botanists is examining the effects of acid rain on the growth of trees and other kinds of plants. We use information gathered from field studies as a basis for experiments performed under controlled laboratory conditions to determine the extent to which various concentrations of acids and heavy metals harm plant growth. Sometimes, our laboratory findings send us back to the field in search of corroborating evidence.

One of the most interesting experiments in our laboratory has demonstrated that exposure to either acid rain or a heavy metal will stunt plants, but when the two are combined (in the form of acidified water to which small amounts of aluminum, copper, lead, or zinc have been added), all plants show sharp declines and the result can be lethal, suggesting a strong synergistic effect. We have carried out tests on many kinds of plants—mosses, bacteria, algae, and fungi, as well as trees. All plants show sharp growth declines.

A common moss used in our laboratory experiments was greatly suppressed under simulated field conditions, and comparative field studies reveal that since the mid 1960s, the coverage of mosses in the Camels Hump forests has declined by 50 percent.

Fungi are another group of plants tested in the laboratory. Necessary to the maintenance of a healthy forest, fungi decompose the piles of leaves and branches that continually fall to the forest floor, recycling nutrients the trees need for continued growth. Healthy tree growth is often also dependent on a complex symbiotic fungus-root association known as mycorrhizae, and the destruction of the sensitive fungal component alone is enough to weaken the tree. Although our researchers have pulled many small spruces from the ground on Camels Hump, we have not been able to find the tiny growths on young roots that are a sign of the mycorrhizal association.

A recent study being done in our laboratory on the wood of spruce trees may provide a clue to one of the most important effects of acid rain. Cores taken from old trees give a record of the ages and yearly growth rates of trees. Sections from the wood cores representing years from the late 1800s onward are analyzed chemically. Preliminary core samples indicate that the content of aluminum in the wood changed very little from the early 1900s until about 1950. At that time, the period associated with the beginnings of acid rain, the concentration of aluminum increased dramatically and in some samples was three times higher than before.

Unlike airborne metal contaminants such as lead, zinc, copper, cadmium, and vanadium, inorganic aluminum is already present in the soil in an insoluble form. Acid rain appears to combine with aluminum, transforming it into a soluble form capable of being taken up by roots. This aluminum is highly toxic, and as it invades the tree, it kills the young roots that supply the tree with water. The tree's water uptake is reduced, causing needles and branches to dry and wither. An experiment carried out in our laboratory demonstrates that spruce trees growing in acidified water to which small amounts of aluminum or cadmium have been added do indeed show a reduction of water uptake. The laboratory plants soon take on the look of the dying spruces in the forest.

Critical work on the effects of aluminum and other aspects of acid rain is also being done by Bernhard Ulrich, a soils scientist at the University of Göttingen, who called the world's attention to the death of spruce and beech trees in Germany. Ulrich estimates that 70 percent of Germany's forests are affected and attributes the cause to acid rain originating in the heavily industrialized Ruhr Valley. Based on studies made over the last sixteen years, he theorizes that the bark and foliage of trees collect low concentrations of sulfates as dry deposition. Acid rains flush the dry acid material from the trees, increasing the acidity of the water reaching the ground. As a result, the levels of soluble aluminum in the soil go up, more and more roots are destroyed, the trees take up less water, the foliage becomes brown, the leaves drop off, and the trees die.

Most of the reports so far of trees presumably damaged by acid rains involve coniferous species. In North America, the spruces are the most dramatic example, but several other conifers are in trouble. Scientists at the University of Pennsylvania and Yale University have produced good evidence that the decline of some coniferous species in the New Jersey Pine Barrens is linked to an increased acidification of the ecosystem. Measurements of the growth rings of pitch, shortleaf, and loblolly pine reveal that these species have experienced substantial and sustained decreases in annual growth rates in the past twenty to thirty years. Black spruces in Maine show a similar downward trend in growth rates.

Conifers seem to be more susceptible than hardwoods to airborne pollution, in part because their needles are exposed year-round to acid rain and other noxious substances. Deciduous trees, which drop their leaves in fall, are given a respite to foliar attack during winter months. Nevertheless, hardwoods may not be immune. From 1965 to the present, the period when the spruces showed a sharp decline, the basal areas of sugar maple and beech growing on the lower slopes of Camels Hump dropped significantly, those of the maples by 15 percent and the beeches by 30 percent. Even more alarming is that the number of maple seedlings and saplings dropped 57 percent. If such losses in only a few years are representative of a general decline in forest productivity, the economic consequences for the lumber industry will be staggering.

In all these grim reports, acid rain is implicated as the villain, but most of the evidence is still circumstantial. Forest environments are complicated, and so are the effects of acid rain. Some red spruce stands in the Northeast, especially those at low elevations, have escaped damage. Controversial studies in Scandinavia indicate that the acidity actually encourages tree growth through the fertilizing action of nitrogen and sulfur. Some Scandinavian scientists claim that their forests now benefit from these added nutrients. They note, however, that the forest soils are losing calcium and magnesium at a fast rate and that any gains may well be short-lived. The puzzle obviously still has many missing pieces, but bit-by-bit the emerging picture shows acid rain to be damaging to forests of many kinds. In some regions, such as Camels Hump, it could be a killer.

Camels Hump
After 1982

After "Catastrophe on Camels Hump" hit the national media, we got busy. We assembled a team of researchers to attack the forest-decline/acid-rain problem head on. In 1983 we measured a 70 percent mortality of red spruce and learned that the boreal forest ecosystem had lost 40 percent of the biomass it had in 1965. Dead spruces littered the upper slopes, and as the forest thinned, strong winds would tear up trees that were still alive. We were dealing with a tragic but intriguing scientific problem because it wasn't clear exactly what was causing these losses. Someone once asked me how I felt about it all and I replied, "It's like watching a snake swallow a frog—it's gruesome but fascinating."

Our new research marked the beginning of a massive study of forest decline that evolved in ways I couldn't have imagined at the outset. There were theories and more theories and debate after debate as to what was causing the decline. Botanists, foresters, pathologists, entomologists, and soil scientists became involved in our work. We knew we had something on Camels Hump that no one else had or could have: the baseline data that Tom Siccama had gathered in the mid-1960s. We could tell exactly how many trees had died, how much forest biomass had been lost, and at what rate the forest was declining. We could show that tree mortality increased with elevation, and soil temperatures rose as the tree canopy disappeared. We had a database that could not be matched anywhere else in the world.

In August of 1984, one of the most unusual field studies ever conducted in this country took place on Camels Hump. It was a joint effort involving the National Aeronautics and Space Administration (NASA), the Jet Propulsion Laboratory (JPL), and the University of Vermont. Scientists at NASA and JPL wanted to learn if remote sensing could be used to detect forest decline, and we had the perfect place for them to find out because we had such extensive information on the condition of the forest for "ground truthing" of their images. Thus began one of the most elaborate field projects I know of.

At one stage of the research, more than forty scientists and technicians, including my son Jim and his wife Ann, were working together on Camels Hump. While some floated balloon markers over the forest, others were engaged in reading sophisticated instruments that recorded light and other radiation measurements. A huge C-130 equipped with all sorts of sensors and computers flew overhead at 17,000 feet while a NASA helicopter hovered just over the forest canopy. Everything was carefully orchestrated to take synchronous measurements of light reflection and absorption. Remarkable images clearly showed the startling extent of forest damage in the Green Mountains.

Later, satellite images demonstrated that the forest decline was primarily on the westerly, windward sides of the mountains and at the higher elevations, which clearly linked the decline we had been watching and measuring with our air-pollution/acid-rain theory. NASA and JPL have since shifted some of their work to include studies of the pollution-ravaged forests of Europe, and it all began on Camels Hump.

German scientists had already been calling attention to the dying forests in Germany and elsewhere in Europe, and now we had shown the same phenomenon occurring here. The media became increasingly interested in our work, and interviews and television appearances soon became regular events. There was widespread concern that what we were seeing on Camels Hump was indeed the devastating effect of air pollution and acid rain, but even if our findings had built a strong case, much of what we were learning remained circumstantial.

In 1986, before the presidential campaign of 1988, I received a call from the office of Gary Hart in Washington. They wanted to know if I would take him up Camels Hump and show him the forest damage that had been reported in the media. Gary Hart was still a leading presidential hopeful when his staff called me, and he was anxious to show his concern for the environment, so I said I would be glad to. Some weeks passed and nothing happened, but there was nothing I could do so I just waited.

Then I received another call asking if I could still lead the hike. When I asked what Gary Hart had in mind, the organizer of the event said he wanted to climb the mountain with me, look at the forest damage, and then give a speech on the environment from the summit of Camels Hump. When I asked who he would be speaking to, the answer was, "The press corps." When I asked how the press corps would get to the summit and the answer was, "They can take the road," I knew I was in trouble. I had to explain that there was no road, and this time there was no answer.

But the whole entourage came anyway. When the day arrived, I met Hart at a commuter parking lot near Interstate 89 and drove to Camels Hump with him. He was lean, well-tanned, and wearing cowboy boots. I was impressed by his knowledge about air pollution and environmental problems in general. Apparently he had worked on congressional committees dealing with the environment and had done his homework. I was pleased to meet such a knowledgeable person and lead him up the mountain I knew so well.

We arrived at 8:00 a.m. and found the press corps already there. Most looked as if they hadn't slept the night before, and they certainly didn't look ready for a three-mile climb up one of Vermont's tallest mountains. But off we went with Hart and me in the lead and about fifteen reporters with cameras and notebooks trailing behind. There was even someone with a television camera along for the adventure. As the hike progressed, I looked back to see how everyone was doing. Hart looked great and was enjoying the climb, but the press corps looked terrible. They were out of shape and already exhausted. I could tell that kind of exercise was clearly not part of their daily routines. As we trudged slowly up the trail, I worried that some in the rear might not make it. There was so much puffing and sweating that I began to feel sorry for the poor souls. I heard a pathetic voice calling out from way back in the line—"When will we be there?"—and I hated to tell them that we weren't even halfway to where I could show them the dying spruces, let alone to the summit.

At that point, one of the organizers realized that we were running out of time because Hart had an afternoon appointment. He said we'd have to turn back before we got to our destination. I was disappointed, but Hart did want to see a dying spruce, so I searched around right where we were and spotted one beside the trail. It had a trunk diameter of about ten inches, and the crown was nearly dead. I announced, "There it is, a dying spruce." Hart stood next to the sad-looking tree, the reporters took notes and shot their photos, and the television camera closed in to record the moment. I had brought an increment corer along and explained that you could tell when a tree had begun to die by looking for the point at which the growth rings began to narrow. We had learned that counting the narrow rings and doing some simple math would correlate the narrowing with the beginning of problems with acid rain.

I gave the corer to Hart, who twisted it into the dying tree. Cameras clicked and the television camera moved in again for another close-up. When he extracted the core, I held my breath hoping it would indeed show the link between the dying spruce and acid rain. Fortunately it was a perfect match. Hart was impressed, and I was relieved that this one spruce growing right beside the trail at a lower elevation represented all the dying spruces the group would have seen higher up on the mountain. Although Gary Hart has since passed as a serious contender for the presidency, Camels Hump still has the "Gary Hart Tree." It is now dead but remains beside the trail as a monument to that famous hike.

The Gary Hart hike was not the last political event on Camels Hump. During the latter part of Ronald Reagan's second term as President, Senator Patrick Leahy asked me to show Reagan's new head of the Environmental Protection Agency, Lee Thomas, the damage done by acid rain. Thomas was, of course, a Republican, and he brought with him the party line that acid rain was not a threat to the environment. The Leahy event dwarfed the Hart hike. In addition to Senator Leahy, the group also included Senator Robert Stafford, who met us at the trailhead but had to remain behind because of a bad hip, and Representative Jim Jeffords. Governor Madeline Kunin also came even though she had recently broken her arm and was wearing a cast. Every step up the mountain was painful for her, but she stayed with us to the very end, and I have admired her ever since.

Again there was the press corps, lots of lots of them, including reporters from all over the country, and more television cameras. I don't even want to think about what it felt like to haul those bulky television cameras and their heavy batteries a couple of miles up the mountain. In addition to all the officials, reporters, and camera crews, nearly a hundred other people who had responded to Senator Leahy's general invitation joined us on the hike.

When we reached the "Gary Hart Tree," I gave the increment corer to Lee Thomas, who proceeded to make a hole near the famous Gary Hart hole. Jim Jeffords was amused and quipped, "Lee, you placed that hole just right—a little above Gary's and to the right."

Camels Hump has played an important role in learning about mountain ecosystems, and the knowledge we have accumulated so far has been used to pass legislation on development and to set clean air standards to protect the environment. More important, Camels Hump is now protected and remains undeveloped. The Camels Hump database, which began with Tom Siccama's dissertation, is unparalleled and continues to provide a baseline for new research. Indeed, recent studies using Siccama's data show that between 1962 and 2005 the deciduous forest moved about four hundred feet upslope as a result of our warming climate. Who knows what discoveries lie ahead?

Acid Rain Then and Now

L ooking back on the early years of our research on Camels Hump, I am struck by how what began as basic ecological research led to some of the best science available on acid rain. The carefully recorded data that Tom Siccama gathered for his doctoral dissertation in the mid-1960s included key information that became extremely useful to us in the late 1970s and 1980s when we noticed that the spruces at higher elevations were dying at an alarming rate. Because we had Siccama's baseline data, we could make the connections and begin to understand what was happening.

During this period, acid rain was being blamed for the acidification of lakes in both the Adirondacks and the Green Mountains. We theorized that our higher elevation forests were being destabilized just as the aquatic ecosystems were. We looked again at Siccama's original data to see what measurable changes had taken place since the mid-1960s. We learned that the acidity of our rain had gone from a normal of pH 5.6 for unpolluted rainwater to a more acidic pH 4. Further, at higher elevations, the fog that bathes trees over one hundred days a year had a pH of about 3, nearly the acidity of vinegar. In addition, we found toxic heavy metals such as copper, zinc, cadmium, arsenic, and vanadium in the soil, along with a poisonous brew of compounds such as DDT and newer concoctions such as polychlorinated biphenyl (PCB) and peroxyacetyl nitrate (PAN).

Our later studies confirmed that, within the timeframe of our combined studies, the forest environment on Camels Hump had changed dramatically, but it was almost impossible for us to prove that acid rain alone was responsible for what we saw happening. Fortunately, the link became stronger when our studies of the chemistry of wood taken from tree cores of 200-year-old sugar maples and spruces revealed that these trees were taking up substances that had not been there before the industrial revolution. Vanadium, arsenic, and cadmium from oil and coal are not found in virgin soils, but they showed up in the wood from our cores and had increased in concentration during post-industrial years.

In the 1970s and 1980s, high elevation forests all the way from the mountains of New England to the mountains of North Carolina were being devastated. Thousands of acres were now covered with dead and dying spruces, looking as if a forest fire had swept the length of the eastern mountains. Camels Hump became the center of worldwide attention because we had Tom Siccama's baseline data to demonstrate the nature and extent of the destruction. Vermont made the headlines, and I remember once when I was on a European lecture tour being asked where I was from. When I said "Vermont," the response was, "Oh, that's where Camels Hump is!" If nothing else, we had succeeded in putting Camels Hump on the map.

When I climbed Camels Hump in 2004, I looked at the upper elevation forest with disbelief. It seemed that a remarkable recovery, in appearance at least, had taken place, with firs having largely replaced the dead spruces. It was hard to remember how damaged the forest appeared twenty-five years ago when we first decided to revisit Tom Siccama's study plots to take new readings. Whether the recovery is permanent or temporary remains to be seen because the high mortality of the weakened spruces was apparently linked to severe winter temperature drops, which have not occurred recently. Our laboratory experiments had shown this correlation between mortality and sudden temperature drops, and now more recent research has added a new concern. It has demonstrated a link between the loss of calcium due to acid rain and the subsequent death of the spruces.

Current studies on the chemistry of rain indicate that in spite of newer clean air standards to reduce sulfur dioxide emissions, the pH of rain has not changed significantly. Whereas sulfuric acid in rain has decreased, nitric acid has increased thanks to nitrogen oxide emissions from automobiles, so there's been little change in the rain's total acidity.

Studies at the U.S. Forest Service's Hubbard Brook Experimental Forest indicate that the addition of nitrogen initially acts as a fertilizer, enhancing tree growth, but the extra growth is accompanied by an increase in cold weather injury because the fertilized trees do not harden off in preparation for winter.

But perhaps the greatest long-term threat to forest health lies in the loss of calcium, now being leached from the soil by acid rain. Forty years of research at Hubbard Brook, which is in northern New Hampshire, has documented that severe losses of calcium are impoverishing forest soils. And calcium cannot be easily replaced because it comes from long-term weathering of parent soil material. The loss of calcium will eventually lower forest productivity, and it remains to be seen what the long-term consequences will be.

Looking back at our research and what we learned over our many years of studying Camels Hump, I see science at its best--fact-based research building on earlier fact-based research as it evolves. At this point in my life, I am humbled by how little we really know about our environment despite everything we've learned. Forest ecosystems are more complex than we can imagine, and many of the interactions between precipitation chemistry, forest soils, and living systems remain unknown. In the words of Frank Egler, "Ecosystems are not only more complex than we think, they are more complex than we can think."

ACKNOWLEDGMENTS

I thank all my good friends and colleagues who have contributed to this book in one way or another, especially Gale Lawrence without whom this book would never have been written. Gale urged me to write about the changing seasons, events in nature, and parts of my life as a botanist. Above all, her encouragement and dedication have been an inspiration for which I am grateful. She also worked tirelessly over the years to put my disorganized papers, slides, and other documents in order so that they could be available for future research in the University of Vermont's Special Collections. My family members have helped reinforce my memories of personal and professional moments and events.

I have also had the benefit of the thoughtful comments and suggestions from a small group of writers and scholars who meet every month to review each other's works. They include Toby and Laura Fulwiler, Rosalind and Carl Andreas, Mike Strauss, Rebecca Sherlock, Glenda Bissex, and Mary Jane Dickerson. I feel fortunate to have had such wonderful support.